Richmond upon Thames Libraries

To renew this item please call the renewals
hotline on 0115 929 3388 or renew online at
www.richmond.gov.uk/libraries

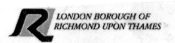

LONDON BOROUGH OF
RICHMOND UPON THAMES

Also by the author:

The Sensuous Slimmer
Caught in the Act
The Single Parent's Survival Guide

THE 15
Minute
RULE

Caroline Buchanan

ROBINSON

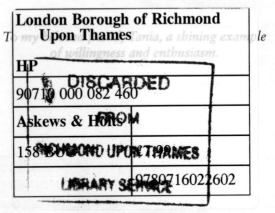
*To my ... Tania, a shining example
of willingness and enthusiasm.*

Constable & Robinson Ltd
55–56 Russell Square
London WC1B 4HP
www.constablerobinson.com

First published in the UK by Robinson,
an imprint of Constable & Robinson Ltd, 2012

ISBN: 978-0-71602-260-2

Printed and bound in the UK

1 3 5 7 9 10 8 6 4 2

MIX
Paper from
responsible sources
FSC® C018072

FOREWORD

by Zelda West-Meads

My first instinct on reading Caroline's brilliant new book, *The 15-Minute Rule*, was that I really must go out and buy a copy for everyone who I thought would find it useful. Then I realized that I would need so many copies that I would probably have to buy a bigger car while I was at it to bring them all home in.

The thing is, everyone could gain something from this book in at least one aspect of their lives. The principle is so simple: the hardest part is getting started, but you can do anything for 15 minutes. And Caroline offers inspirational advice on doing exactly that: tackling anything by breaking tasks down to 15-minute chunks and simply getting started.

It is written with great warmth and humour, and manages not to be preachy or judgemental. There is no assumption that you have to be superwoman (or man) to be able to make changes in your life, and from the small tasks such as sorting out a cluttered room, to the larger ones, such as mending a broken heart, they are all treated with the same respect.

And over and above the very practical and straightforward advice, Caroline has also drawn on her many years of experience as a Relate counsellor to offer fascinating insights and help with emotional problems in her chapters on relationships, friends and family.

An extremely useful book that many people will want to

read and then keep on their shelves to dip into time and again whenever they need a friendly pep-talk on any aspect of their life that's bothering them.

CONTENTS

Introduction: The 15-Minute Rule   1

1   How it Works   3

2   The Myth of Willpower   15

3   Pulverizing Procrastination   25

4   Willingness and Enthusiasm   48

5   Your ACE Card   60

6   Weighty Matters   69

7   Your Love Life   84

8   Your Career   110

9   Finding Financial Freedom   124

10   Friends and Family   137

11   Getting the Glow, Inside and Out   153

12   Conclusion   164

Acknowledgements   168

INTRODUCTION:

THE 15-MINUTE RULE

Can you spare 15 minutes? Do you want to become a more motivated, productive person? Do you want to make your dreams come true? Then this book is for you.

The 15-Minute Rule is a lifestyle tool that can work for anyone. It is designed to deal with all the tasks we put off and which then become such heavy weights to carry around. Focusing your attention for just 15 minutes at a time is something anyone can do. It can help you to tackle all the things you don't want to deal with, the things you run away from, put off or ignore at your peril – all those irritating little chores that can give you a big headache: the shopping, the uncomfortable phone calls, the housework, office hassles and even the dreaded paperwork.

Before I go any further may I first say congratulations to you for picking up this book. You are obviously someone who is willing to try something new. Whether you are keen and motivated to change or are using the escape of a good read to put off some evil chore that is screaming for your attention, then this is the book is for you.

The 15-Minute Rule is going to change your life.

If procrastination is your enemy, you are about to learn how to overcome it. All the problems you feel you are avoiding or resisting can be resolved with the minimum of effort and leave you free from fear, anxiety, exhaustion, misery and all the other balls and chains you drag along behind you. Once you learn how to get started, you will be amazed at how easy it is to get on top of those undone chores. You'll even find your energy levels rising dramatically.

And following the 15-Minute Rule is fun! All your must-dos can be tackled with a much lighter heart. The method is tried and tested and the results speak for themselves. The essence of the Rule is extremely simple:

YOU CAN DO ALMOST ANYTHING FOR 15 MINUTES AT A TIME

1

HOW IT WORKS

This book actually started with a 15-minute commitment. I was about to tackle one of my ghastliest chores of the year – my tax return. Like most people, I loathe paperwork and the anxiety attached to this particular task was hideous. I would have done pretty much anything to avoid it. Pairing socks was always a good one – my husband's, my daughter's, mine, all lying at the bottom of the ironing basket, which was where I'd left them until I had nothing better to do than to sort them out.

At times like this, all kinds of jobs suddenly seemed vital but sock pairing was definitely in the top ten, as was washing the kitchen floor, making sure I hadn't thrown away anything important, making that telephone call to the friend I've been meaning to call for ages, or phoning the gas man for a service. These things need to be done! They're important! Well, yes, they are, but they're not going to help you get the tax return done.

Procrastination, though, just makes the thought of the job that much worse; it starts assuming nightmare proportions. All the dreaded 'What ifs?' start creeping in: What if I can't do my tax? What if I can't get it done on time? What if I'm fined? What if I can't pay it? What if I get sent to prison? What will happen to my family if I'm locked up? How will I cope with jail? Will the uniform suit me? Oh, yes, our imaginations can run riot, round and round and hither and thither when anxiety takes over.

So how did I solve the tax-return problem? I couldn't keep ignoring it and hoping it would go away forever. I didn't have a choice, and decided to give it just 15 minutes. Anything would be a start. But when? The deadline was fast approaching. It would have to be today. Well maybe tomorrow.

Yes, tomorrow would be good.

And guess what? Tomorrow came and was suddenly today, and I couldn't put it off any longer.

All the procrastination had given me a rotten headache. It was 10 a.m. I took a couple of painkillers and decided to start at 2 p.m. I felt a tiny bit of relief once I'd set the time for action but the headache didn't budge. There was so much to do and I knew I really should be getting on with it. So, I decided to bring it forward an hour and finally it was time for lift-off.

Surprise, surprise, it was much easier than I'd thought it would be. By the time I had pulled together a few relevant bits of information and set up and dated the document I was done for the day. I felt peaceful. My headache had vanished. My anxiety had plummeted. I had my perspective back! I also had my energy back. At this rate I knew I'd have it finished by the end of the week – it was only Tuesday and a few more 15-minute sessions would see the job through.

As the week progressed I found the subsequent 15-minute sessions were a lot easier to start than the first one. Because I had already begun I no longer had the head-banging, screaming frustrations of trying to locate all the relevant pieces of paper that you need for a tax return. They were already in place. The second 15 minutes was beautifully straightforward – the feeling of being overwhelmed had completely disappeared. The third 15 minutes was a breeze and the final 15 minutes saw the job checked and completed.

I felt wonderfully relieved, and I've found it much easier to do my tax return ever since. I'm not saying it's my favourite job in the world but it's so much more manageable than it ever was. It still has the potential to irritate me but I know I can nip it in the bud by going back to my Rule and spending just 15 minutes on getting the process started.

Those first 15 minutes are for laying the vital foundation stone which is the beginning of the end of the horrible task. Indeed, with some jobs, one session of 15 minutes may turn out to be all you need to complete the whole thing.

To get us started, here's an inspiring quotation from the author Thomas Carlyle. It's worth writing out, pinning up or placing it somewhere obvious so that you can refer to it regularly.

> 'Our main business is not to see what lies dimly at a distance, but to do what lies clearly at hand.'

Carlyle also said: 'The best effect of any book is that it excites the reader to self-activity.'

And I sincerely believe this is what the 15-Minute Rule can do for you.

CHASING DREAMS AND MAKING DECISIONS

The 15-Minute Rule is not just about dealing with the tricky things you have left undone. It is also about embracing all those dreams you long to become reality. The thing to remember is that you really can do almost anything for 15 minutes. For example, if a sixty-year-old woman wants to become a ballet dancer, why shouldn't she? Just 15 minutes a day in a tutu learning the basic ballet positions is possible. It might not lead to a starring role in the next production of *Swan Lake*, but it could allow her to express a love of dance while improving her health, confidence and joie de vivre.

It's an extreme example, perhaps, but I'm a great believer in following your passion. If you long to become a best-selling novelist, a star of stage and screen, a highly respected academic, a famous artist, a successful musician and so on, then you really need to give it a go. If the passion is there then follow it. We can't do everything but we can improve our well-being if we combine our passion with our talents.

Here's another quote that I love. It's a line from the film *Terms of Endearment* and is spoken by the character played by Shirley MacLaine:

> 'Work like you don't need the money
> Love like your heart has never been broken
> And dance like no one is watching.'

And what about the other big things in life? Do you want to find love or dramatically improve the relationship you already have? How are your finances – is there room for improvement? Do you want to lose weight? Do you want to create positive new habits? Stop obsessing? Banish worry? Would you like oodles of confidence, and to learn to love yourself?

Are you trying to pluck up the courage to step outside your comfort zone? Do you long to make the most of your potential?

How about decision making? Is it difficult for you? Do opportunities pass you by or do you grab them with both hands? How is your goal-setting technique? Or have you put that task off until another day too?

Whatever it is you want or need, why not try the 15-Minute Rule? You have nothing to lose and plenty to gain.

There's only one thing holding you back from your dreams. And that is you. Not the core of you, the essence of you, but your distorted beliefs about yourself – the old tapes in your head that are giving you false or outdated messages. The tapes that go round and round on an endless loop saying things like: 'I'm not good enough'; 'I couldn't possibly'; 'I don't deserve it'; 'It's too scary'; 'I haven't got the time'; 'It's not my thing'; 'I'm just lazy', etc.

Now is the time to update your internal technology and switch to a positive message.

One of my dear friends is a highly inspirational woman who embraces change; she told me that she thinks of a negative thought as a groove in a record, one that we deepen when we imagine worst-case scenarios. For some time now she has been working at overlaying those grooves by imagining the complete opposite – the best-case scenarios.

So why not try it? Replace each negative thought with a positive one and keep practising until you get the hang of it and it starts to become second nature. No more plaguing yourself with negative 'What if . . . things become really difficult?'; instead, concentrate on the positive 'What if . . . things become wonderfully straightforward?'

So how about trying this positive 'What if?' What if you commit to embracing the 15-Minute Rule? It really is a win-win situation. As Ralph Waldo Emerson said:

> 'What lies behind us and what lies before us are tiny matters compared to what lies within us.'

THE UNEXPECTED GLITCH

We are all horribly aware of the jobs we just don't want to do. On top of that, problems often crop up that we haven't anticipated. If we're not careful this sort of thing can throw a huge spanner into the workings of our day but the extent to which it derails our plans is up to us. We can react badly to it or we can react well. The choice is ours. And if we feel emotional about what happens – even if we simply feel annoyance – we're more likely to react badly.

'But it made me feel terrible!' we might say, as an excuse for our day getting completely out of hand.

Or worse still, 'My day is ruined now!' Of course, nine times out of ten, the day is not ruined. And it doesn't mean that everything else that day is going to go wrong. The truth is that we can restart our day at any time, telling ourselves, 'From now on, my day is going to be a good one!'

It's no use panicking about how to deal with the unexpected, and worrying about the time we won't be spending on what we had originally planned. Why? Because there's a problem, and we have to deal with it. Perhaps we feel angry, especially if we're trying to keep lots of plates spinning in the air, and anticipate the hours we will have to spend trying to sort it all out.

But not if you adopt the 15-Minute Rule. If you know this problem is only going to take 15 minutes to resolve or at least partially resolve, you are less likely to waste hours fretting about it and running around ineffectively like a headless chicken.

Devote just 15 minutes to focusing on what you can do about it even if, ultimately, it's going to take a bit longer. For a good start, focus on the solution rather than the problem and try to let go of any resentment the problem might have created. Brainstorm solutions and get cracking. You may find you resolve the whole thing with time to spare.

WHY IT WORKS

One of the reasons my 15-Minute Rule works is that you get to suspend any muddled thinking while you get on and just *do* your 15 minutes. The instructions are clear, concise and not open to manipulation and it appeals to both the disorganized and the organized.

It's a tool that is made up of imagination, positive thinking, fun, focus and creativity. It also happens to follow the SMART goal-setting rules: Specific, Measurable, Achievable, Realistic and Time-phased.

The 15-Minute Rule also has elements of a therapy known as Cognitive Behavioural Therapy, which is used by psychologists to treat many emotional and psychological problems. This therapy changes the way you feel by changing how you think (cognitive) and what you do (behaviour). By using these techniques, you can start to conquer negative emotions such as misplaced fear, as well as addressing self-defeating behaviour such as avoidance. So, you can see how this relates to the 15-Minute Rule where we change how we feel (anxious, guilty about putting things off) by changing how we behave (we spend 15 minutes doing it).

The 15-Minute Rule is flexible, and appeals to those who want instant gratification, who want everything *now*, and also the longer-term players who recognize the benefits of consistency and persistence.

Whichever camp you're in, it can give you the opportunity to explore all kinds of ideas until you find projects, passions and activities that really suit you.

When you commit to those 15 minutes you will find yourself completely focused on the task at hand. Even if you're floundering about what to do first, you will still be focused. You will find that you want to get on with it and will naturally use the time to its best advantage because you know it will only be for 15 minutes.

Never forget that laying the foundation stone will underpin the whole project. Whatever you actually achieve, you will at the very least have made a commitment. No matter how busy you are, or however lazy or stressed you might be feeling, 15 minutes is manageable, especially when you reward yourself afterwards. Virtue, of course, will be an automatic reward and it will go a long way towards making you feel good because you will feel a sense of relief – and maybe real joy – that your project has been started. The good feelings may actually feel out of proportion to the 15 minutes. You may wonder why you're feeling so fantastic after such a short time investment. But does it matter? It's entirely natural to feel good about yourself when you know you've sown the seed that has the potential to bring great rewards, even if that reward is simply peace of mind.

Both small and large gains can be made with the 15-Minute Rule, and each can bring enormous satisfaction and a hefty boost to your self-esteem.

THE SECRET SIX

The 15-Minute Rule is made up of six stages that will help
you with whatever you wish to achieve. For larger creative and
constructive projects take note of each one of them; for smaller
tasks you may find that you need only the first 15 minutes to
get yourself started and possibly the task over and done with.

One: Be Inspired

Copy out the following quotation and pin it up where you will
see it several times a day:

> 'Whatever you do, or dream you can do, begin it –
> boldness has genius, power and magic in it. Begin it
> now.'
>
> Goethe

Two: Visualize

Close your eyes and imagine yourself just as you've completed
your chosen goal. Feel it, taste it, touch it. You are more likely to
reach your goal if you visualize being there. Next, write down
your goal in a safe place: a brand new file on your computer,
for example, or in a notebook bought especially for the purpose. Writing it down will help you to see it, store the thought
of it in your memory and also greatly increase the chances of
your achieving it. Visualize, visualize, visualize.

Three: Plan

If you haven't started already, pick a time to begin. How about
now? Or some time within the next three days? You must be
able to find just 15 minutes out of those seventy-two hours.
Once you have picked a start time, stick to it; commit to it.
If you wait until you feel motivated, it won't get done. If you

conquer the behaviour that leads to procrastination then, regardless of your mood, the thinking and feeling will catch up.

Four: Prepare

It's all in the preparation. Read this book, become inspired and you are well on your way to making those dreams come true. Take note of the section on willingness and enthusiasm, which will serve you extraordinarily well by giving you an extra boost. As you read, imagine all the positive changes that you could embrace and write down any ideas that occur to you. You can sift through them later and see which ones have real appeal.

Five: The 15-Minute Rule

Time to implement the 15-Minute Rule. Pick your chosen task, set your watch and start timing. These 15 minutes will include everything – for example, turning on the computer and waiting for it to warm up and getting comfortable in your chair. Now, if necessary, brainstorm. Write down anything and everything that occurs to you regarding your chosen project: sentences, phrases, words, drawings – whatever will speak to you when you look at it again. Stick with your task. Making a cup of tea at this stage is to be avoided. Focus on what you need to do, avoid all distractions, apart from emergencies, and simply get on with it. If nothing much is happening then brainstorm further. Do anything that will help you achieve something! When the 15-minutes is up – stop!

Even if you are eager to go on, stop. Stick to your boundary. This gives you the important message that you can trust yourself. You said 15 minutes, so 15 minutes it will be. It will also be much easier to come back to the project if you have left it while feeling full of enthusiasm, and possibly wanting more time.

When you've finished you are likely to feel so much better than you did just a quarter of an hour previously. You might not believe where the time has gone. How are you feeling?

Relieved? Excited? Hopeful? Now savour the experience and enjoy every moment of your accomplishment. Bask in those rewarding feelings. By doing this, you will be creating good memories that will inspire and strengthen your motivation for your future 15-minute sessions.

Once you've grasped the whole idea of the 15-Minute Rule, you can tailor-make it just for you. But don't run before you can walk. After your first segment, I suggest your next two 15-minute sessions are done within a three-day period. In seventy-two hours you can definitely manage three lots of 15 minutes. Of course you will eventually be 'allowed' to spend as much time as you'd like on your particular project but only when you're really into it. The moment you get stuck or bored, go straight back to the 15-Minute Rule and follow this until you feel raring to go again.

Another wonderful thing about the 15-Minute Rule is that a lot of work goes on subconsciously and effortlessly in between sessions. Your project is lodged in your brain and your brain is still thinking about it even when you're doing something completely different and not aware that you're thinking about it.

Six: Reward Yourself

Pat yourself on the back for each step and celebrate your victories large and small. Rewards are important.

Make a list of various treats that are easily accessible – anything from reading a chapter of your new book, watching a television programme (even if it's a recording or a download), lying down and listening to some favourite music, planning a trip of a lifetime.

WHAT'S BEEN STOPPING YOU?

Are you frightened of failure? Or frightened of success? Perhaps it's both? Either way those fears present an obstacle.

Remember what Susan Jeffers said: 'Feel the fear and do it anyway.' Taking action is better than lying around doing nothing; it's when that sense of having achieved nothing kicks in that we feel low, stressed, anxious and are more likely to beat ourselves up.

You can avoid feeling like that if you just get on with it and do your 15 minutes. Please, please don't wait until you feel ready to start! You could end up waiting forever.

According to William James, the nineteenth-century psychologist and philosopher, and the father of the modern day self-help book:

> 'Action seems to follow feeling, but really action and feeling go together; and by regulating the action, which is under the more direct control of the will, we can indirectly regulate the feeling, which is not.'

FIRING UP YOUR POTENTIAL

The tried-and-tested examples in this book will hopefully inspire you to strive for your goals. Of course achievement is wonderful for self-esteem and confidence, and for every 15-minute commitment you make you'll see that it gets easier and easier to achieve. You will actually be creating new habits, many of which will eventually become second nature to you.

You will also find the tools to help you give up some of your bad procrastination habits, which you've spent so much time and energy practising, over and over again, and telling yourself you're going to stop, also over and over again . . . Practice makes perfect and boy are we good at practising bad habits! Einstein had it about right: 'Insanity: doing the same thing over and over again and expecting different results.'

BEATING BAD HABITS

There is a technique called 'surfing' that's used to tackle addictions and which lends itself brilliantly to the 15-Minute Rule. What stops so many people from tackling an addiction is the fear that their cravings will become overwhelming when they quit. But when the craving 'wave' hits, you can distract yourself by doing something, anything, other than give in to your addiction, the bad habit. Committing 15 minutes to doing something else will keep you busy, and hopefully by then the craving will have passed. If not, you can repeat the process by spending another 15 minutes on a second task. Cravings do not last – they are temporary. And each time you surf a wave, and ride it out, you will reinforce your new good behaviour until, before too long, this new good habit takes the place of the old destructive one.

For the scientific among you, one of the reasons the 15-Minute Rule works is that activity promotes vitality. There is an area of the brain called the reticular activating system (RAS), which is a complex network of nerve connections that has a role in our ability to be alert and wakeful. Activity in the extensive nervous system connecting our brain with our bodies stimulates the RAS. Simply put, the more active we are, the more alert we feel. Activity promotes well-being, which feels good, and this then leads us to want to do more activity. It is a constructive circle, and when you change your behaviour patterns you are cutting out a lot of the dead wood in your life to make room for all the good new stuff. Commit to 15 minutes, and be inspired:

> 'The moment one definitely commits oneself,
> Then Providence moves too.
> All sorts of things occur to help one
> That would never otherwise have occurred.'
>
> Goethe

2

THE MYTH OF WILLPOWER

'Sometimes your only available transportation
is a leap of faith.'
                                    Margaret J. Shepherd

Let me tell you something exciting: willpower is a myth. A con-troversial statement perhaps, but I'll say it again: willpower is a myth, and you can stop worrying right now about whether or not you have it, or indeed can summon it up when you most need it.

We have free will, yes, although some of us may sometimes find that hard to believe. Many people find it baffling that they can be extremely determined in some areas of their life and passive in others. And they interpret this passivity as a failure to summon up willpower. But willpower is not something that can be summoned up; it is an illusion. So, what is the difference between thinking, 'I know I ought to but it's just so hard' and 'I'm going to do this and nothing's going to stop me'? The secret is that . . .

DETERMINATION COMES FROM A
SETTLED DECISION

Making a settled decision is so powerful. It will help you take the first big step towards flipping the feeling of 'I know I ought to' into 'I'm going to do this now come what may.' Let's now explore what it is that helps bring about that change.

'I know I ought to' smacks of ambivalence. It immediately highlights the dilemma of knowing that you should do something, while feeling reluctant to do it. When we feel ambivalent about a project we are far more likely to either abandon it altogether or put it on the back burner. You will probably revisit the dilemma frequently, each time telling yourself 'I know I ought to,' but still getting nowhere. More energy wasted!

And, as the saying goes, if you keep on doing what you keep on doing, you'll keep on getting what you keep on getting.

Talk to reformed smokers and many of them will say they tried to give up many times before they succeeded. Some even bought into the myth that they just couldn't summon up the willpower to sustain it all those previous times but then, one day, bingo, they had success.

'All my unsuccessful attempts at giving up were part of my journey towards being a non-smoker,' said a friend. Well, yes, that is absolutely true, but making a settled decision is likely to make your journey less troublesome.

We are able to make some settled decisions because they concern the ambition just ahead of us, that future better person we're going to become. These are the easy decisions such as: 'Should I treat myself for all that hard work?' or 'I will go for that job because I am so right for it.' If we don't have mixed feelings about something then the correct course of action is more obvious, and it's then easier to make a decision about what to do. For example, here are two statements without a question mark in sight: 'I've decided I'm going to go for that promotion, I deserve it' and 'I'm definitely going to ask my partner to think about booking a romantic holiday. It will do us good.' You may still feel some anxiety, when you've made the decision, but at this point you're prepared to deal with it in order to pursue your goals.

However, if you have some ambivalence about something, such as losing weight before a romantic beach holiday, you may have more trouble deciding on a course of action. You know that if you lose those excess pounds you'll be healthier, slimmer and fitter and your confidence and self-esteem may benefit too. What's more, your immediate incentive is buying a new swimsuit and looking good on the beach! Yes, you can see all the pluses and are hard pushed to find any minuses.

But then self-sabotage, the dreaded enemy creeps in: 'I've dieted a thousand times – it doesn't work!' or 'I'll start next Monday.' Or 'It's not fair – I have such a slow metabolism' and 'There won't be enough time before the holiday to lose what I need to lose.' Needless to say, you're not going to lose the weight if you keep indulging in these kinds of negative thoughts. But if you decide to do something differently, for instance join a slimming club, there could be a very different outcome. Many dieters find clubs and groups such as WeightWatchers, LighterLife, Slimming World very helpful. But it's not just the information, the weekly weigh-in, the power of the group, the common goal, the support and inspiration that can work wonders: it's the commitment. When you enrol in one of these programmes you have made a settled decision. And you were halfway to the goal when you walked through the door on the first visit.

So, willpower is not a magic wand that you do or do not possess. When you think about it seriously, what actually is willpower? If used in a positive way it's just another name for self-discipline, albeit one that is loaded with pressure. When the rewards are immediate and obvious, self-discipline is a doddle.

For example, if I asked you to take a 15-minute walk up a steep hill where there's a winning lottery ticket waiting for you, with no strings attached, do you think you would find the discipline to start walking? If I asked you to hike up there to do my pile of ironing – for nothing – you might not feel so motivated! Even if there were no reward of the winning lottery ticket, nor any chore at the end like the ironing, you may feel you are extremely lacking in the self-discipline department. But are you? Look at the evidence. Even if you are going through a very lazy period there will be certain things that you do every day that require self-discipline. Getting up, showering, getting dressed, having breakfast and cleaning your teeth are all pretty necessary, but don't forget that you are still actively choosing to do these things. They come easily to you because you see them as must-do tasks and with constant practice they have become almost automatic.

You manage most of your must-dos because your decision is made for you. Now look at all the things you can do, and do regularly. Cooking an evening meal from scratch, perhaps, or tidying up your surroundings? Most of the time you will choose to do these things because the benefits are obvious to you: enjoyment from the cooking, feeling more relaxed in a tidy home. These may seem easy compared to the longer-term tasks that require work now for a pay-off later; this can weaken your self-discipline. It's a bit like gardening. You have to plant the seeds if you want to eventually smell the flowers and eat the fruit!

So how best to make a settled decision? As with any choice there will be perceived gains and losses. Let's get back to that romantic beach holiday for a moment. On the one hand you can see the healthy and toned body that can be yours and on the other hand you can see weeks or months of depriving yourself of all the food and drinks you love, which makes it seem an impossible dream and not worth the pain of all that deprivation.

This is the point where it would be worth shaking up your kaleidoscope to take a different view. Rather than weigh up the pros and cons daily, and achieving nothing, you could do something else: you could employ the 15-Minute Rule!

The first 15-minute session could be used to start brain-storming all the advantages of reaching a healthy weight. The next 15-minute session could be spent rewriting your negative thoughts into positive ones, for instance, changing 'My target weight is an impossible dream' into 'My target weight is completely possible. I really can make this dream come true.'

One of the many joys of the 15-Minute Rule is that once you decide to do it you no longer feel resentment, which will disappear as if waved away by that magic wand. Even the most tedious and tricky jobs become less irritating when you frame them within a 15-minute time slot.

HOW TO MAKE A GOOD DECISION

Many people find making decisions extremely hard, even if they're small decisions such as choosing from a restaurant menu. But whether it's marriage or divorce, fish or fowl, what underpins all that angst is the fear of loss. If we didn't have to give up something in order to try to gain something better, we wouldn't have a problem with making decisions. If I asked you to choose between being rich or poor you are quite likely to plump for rich. Even if it were not a snap decision you would still, after weighing everything up, probably choose rich. If your social conscience pricks you could comfort yourself with the thought that you could give it all away. But actually you might want to consider the advantages of not being rich. You wouldn't be inundated with begging letters. Potential partners wouldn't want to marry you just for your money. You may not have a family feud over your will. Instead you would feel secure that you're loved for yourself.

Some good decisions are made while in a pit of despair but others require a more measured thought process. Be aware of your emotional state when you're trying to make a decision.

If you're crying your eyes out because your abusive partner has betrayed you yet again, and then you get a moment of clarity when you realize you have to get out of the relationship, build on that. This is the split second when you become aware that this time you could do something differently. Keep that awareness going just a few seconds longer and you could make a big change for the better.

Don't do what you've done a hundred times before: a couple of days go by, you forgive your partner, you hope your trust can be rebuilt (again), you feel a bit better, you begin to get your equilibrium back and then you're betrayed again. The pattern is firmly established.

Some good decisions are blindingly obvious. But as for the rest of them, the ones that leave you pulling your hair out or going round and round in circles, here are some suggestions that will help you make a calm and settled decision:

- Start with the 15-Minute Rule! Try not to go round and round in endless spirals of indecision. Over-thinking is not good for you. Give yourself this time to mull over your options and trust your gut instinct.

- Acknowledge the fear of what you might lose. Would it be so bad? Presumably you're looking for improvement so you might have to let go of the old behaviour to make way for the new. Remember that when one door shuts, other doors open. The fear of missing out can keep you in a quagmire of unnecessary chaos. You cannot have it all. Accept that you may have to miss out on some things in order to achieve your goal.

- Accept that you can't have total certainty, no matter how much you might want it. One of life's very few guarantees is that things change, whether you like it or not.

- Remember that NOT making a decision is in fact making a decision. You are choosing not to act. And in doing so you can invite a lot of needless pain and worry. Over-analyzing and obsessing can be crippling.

- When you're trying to make a serious or life-changing decision, make sure you're in a reasonable frame of mind. Centre yourself, avoid alcohol or stimulants and try to make sure you're not too tired. If you are feeling slightly tipsy or too exhausted, your perspective will be skewed and things will look very different in the morning.

- While it may be a good idea to seek advice and talk things through with others you do not need to base your decision on the opinions of other people. Trust yourself. We are our own experts! We do not need to rely on someone else to make our decisions.
- Watch out for people-pleasing. Do not base your decisions entirely around someone else. Of course we have to consider how a decision will affect others, but don't sabotage yourself in the process.
- Try the circle trick. At the top of a piece of paper, write down the question you want to answer. Then draw a diagram. Draw three circles; a large one, medium one within that and then a smaller one within that.

In the outer circle write the circumstances surrounding your decision.

In the middle circle write what your head is telling you.

In the inner circle write what your heart is telling you.

You will find the first two quite easy, but it's the core circle that can be a little bit scary.

Try to face the fear and listen to your inner voice; it really will help you come to a settled decision.

- Remember that things are often not set in stone. If you fear you've made the wrong decision then you can learn from your mistakes, reverse the decision or, if that's not possible, accept the consequences and move on.

THE POWER OF THREE

Another effective trick, which can be used alongside the 15-Minute Rule, is to divide chores into threes. For example, I sometimes deal with three bits of admin a day, tidy three things in the sitting room and make three telephone calls before lunch.

We like to think in threes: beginning, middle, end; mind, body, spirit; the Holy Trinity.

I know I'm not the only person who likes the number three. It seems concise, constructive and productive. And when used with the 15-Minute Rule you will be amazed at what it can achieve.

Take my kitchen table, which like many other kitchen tables across the land is often heaving with 'Things to do'. I'll tell you what I see when I look at mine right now: my laptop, mobile, landline telephone, vitamins, three piles of papers that need sorting, hand cream, make-up mirror, notepad, notebook, dog treats (two packets), a jug of wilting daffodils, a list of telephone numbers, a shopping list, nail varnishes (five), radio, cockerel doorstop (moved out of the way because my dog has been chewing it), newspaper cuttings, kitchen roll, and a mug of cold tea – phew!

Clearing up this lot will take time, but not if I do it in threes. I will now clear up three things and time it . . . That took twenty seconds. I put the telephone back in its cradle, slugged back the cold tea, put the mug in the dishwasher and tidied away the dog treats. I still can't see the wood for the trees but I am beginning to feel a lovely sense of order creeping in. And wait! I can see bits of the table again! I'm feeling inspired and motivated.

Using the Power of Three alongside the 15-Minute Rule, even if it's using three sessions of 15 minutes each, can transform housework and make it much more manageable.

I was staying in a cottage for a week recently and when it was over the time for the final clear-up arrived. I had books and papers everywhere on top of all the usual household stuff. I decided to spend 15 minutes on the kitchen, 15 on the sitting room and 15 on the dining room where I had been working. I was a whirling dervish and with all that activity, thanks to the brain's RAS which we learned about earlier (see page 14), I was full of vim and vigour when I finished forty-five minutes later.

You can be as creative as you like with your threes and, as with anything, the more you practise the easier it will be. It comes very naturally to me now, and it is a constructive habit I want to hang on to. I use it for pretty much anything; for example, I might need to have a tricky discussion later, but instead of fretting about what to say and what not to say, I apply my Power of Three rule and just concentrate on three aspects that I feel need to be talked about.

You can use the Power of Three in any sort of division: three tasks, three days, three months, three different projects to have on the go using your 15-Minute Rule, such as learning Italian, clearing out the broom cupboard, and writing a novel. Work with three in any way that grabs you.

FEAR OF FAILURE

There are always going to be people who won't try anything outside their comfort zone because they fear failure. But really, the only failure is not trying. 'The only place where success comes before work is in the dictionary,' said Vince Lombardi, the legendary football coach. That's true, but on the other hand it might also suggest that failure doesn't require any effort. But doing nothing is exhausting. Think of all the energy you spend stressing about the things you mean to achieve. Or the energy you spend trying not to worry about something. If you're feeling exhausted, miserable, depressed or unmotivated, doing nothing can seem very appealing. But if you keep on doing nothing, you will only get more of the same. If you want to feel better then you need to try something else.

Use the 15-Minute Rule and do three things within that time frame. Even if it's just taking a dirty coffee cup to the kitchen, making one telephone call and going to find that book you're reading, you will feel some improvement. Positivity breeds positivity. Activity breeds activity and promotes vitality.

SUMMARY

So, now you know that willpower is a myth there's no need to waste your time beating yourself up for something none of us has. However, what we all do have is the ability to make a settled decision. The Power of Three and the 15-Minute Rule will help you do this, and to achieve your goals as a result.

3

PULVERIZING PROCRASTINATION

'Whether you THINK YOU CAN
Or think you can't
YOU'RE RIGHT.'

I have this quote on a card on my kitchen notice board. It's
often attributed to Henry Ford. But whoever said it, it's so true!
Just try it for yourself right now. Turn your thoughts to something you feel ambivalent or unsure about. Think CAN, and
then think CAN'T and see how differently you feel.

It goes back to one of the basic principles of Cognitive
Behavioural Therapy (CBT): how we think affects how we feel.
And we can change the way we think.

As an example, let's take a difficult conversation you might
need to have, possibly with your partner. We'll start with
CAN'T: 'I can't do it. It will only lead to a row. I can't face it.
I hate confrontation. It might hurt him/her and I really don't
want that. He/she might leave me if I bring this up.'

Now we'll do it with CAN: 'I can do it. It might lead to an
argument but I can handle that. I can deal with the outcome,
whatever it is. The stress of pretending this issue doesn't exist
is not doing either of us any good. It might hurt him/her but it's
the truth. If our relationship suffers because of this, I can cope.
Or at least I have friends who can help me cope.'

It's a natural phenomenon to avoid those things we do not wish to face. But just think about the amount of energy you spend in doing just that. Not long ago I was putting off writing a letter that I had to send but which I had spent weeks avoiding. But then I was away for a week, and without my usual distractions I was determined to do the task before I returned home. Still, though, I kept putting it off. It hung over me like a big cloud, nudging me whenever I tried to forget about it. I got on with other things, and then nudge, nudge, it kept on interfering with my enjoyment. 'Oh go away, I'll do you tomorrow,' I thought. I ended up dreaming about it and woke with it hanging over me in the morning, and throughout the next day. Finally, one damp afternoon, I sat at the kitchen table and set the egg-timer for 15 minutes.

It was done in eight! But in the days before I'd been carrying around a tonne of angst about it. I had thought it would be a difficult letter to write. But all that angst for eight minutes of doing something that had to be done?

Why had I wasted so much energy? Perfectionism. I kept thinking, 'It has to be right! It has to be spot on. It has to be perfect.' Which was just crazy. The letter had to be written, perfect or not. And of course it could never actually be perfect because I'm only human. That's something to keep in mind. Doing our best is all we can aim for, and settling for good enough is better than doing nothing at all. Reasons for procrastination are many and varied but unless you're bone idle most of them will stem from an emotional reaction. Fear of failure, fear of success, fear of missing out, fear of not being responsible enough, fear of not coping, fear of what you might find, fear of anger, guilt, sadness, boredom – whatever it is that's stopping you getting on will almost certainly have fear behind it. The fear won't disappear if you avoid tackling the task that is causing you to feel that way. Plus, your inability to take action could lead to further fears over the consequences of doing nothing.

The other day I read a report that said procrastination in society is getting worse. And, similarly, after ten years on a research project that should have taken half that time, an industrial psychologist found that procrastination was not only on the increase but also makes people poorer, fatter and unhappier! I could have told you that in one minute, from personal experience alone!

According to research company ICD, 85 per cent of us own up to procrastinating every day. And well over a quarter of a million people a year get fined for sending in late tax returns!

The only way out is through: you can't ignore it; you can't go round it; you have to go through it.

There is no way out of doing your tax, for example. It has to be done. Most of us have to fight to overcome procrastination and face our fears on this one. Fines have risen steeply for those who don't manage to meet the deadline. But every single person I've asked to try the 15-Minute Rule to help them tackle their tax return has been amazed at how painless it is.

CASE STUDY: SARAH

Sarah, a freelance designer, had been delaying completing her tax return for months before she heard about the 15-Minute Rule.

'I'd put off doing it for about six months,' she said. 'I kept saying "I'm going to do it, I'm going to do it" but I didn't! I had just gone freelance that year so this was the first time I'd had to fill it in with this new way of working and I'd heard so many things that had put me off, such as how complicated it was. So, rather than just do it, I got more and more stressed and worked up about it. I was sticking my head in the sand and I couldn't face it.

'Suddenly it was too late, and I thought possibly too expensive, to get an accountant to help me and I realized I had to do it by myself. I'd heard all these horrible rumours about the self-assessment forms, such as how the tax office computer system was going to crash, and this didn't help my mood at all.

'The deadline was imminent and I was constantly reminded about it by advertisements on TV, telling me I didn't have much time left.

'Eventually, I thought I'd apply the rule and give it 15 minutes – simply to put my mind at rest.'

Sarah set the clock, went upstairs and turned the computer on, filled in a couple of sections of the form and then found that her time was up.

After going downstairs for a quick break, she felt so pleased with herself that she went back up and did another 15 minutes.

She finished it the following day. 'I cannot get over how easy it was in the end,' she said.

It's easy to procrastinate when a job isn't that urgent. These are more likely to be put on the backburner but, unless they're tackled, they will probably catch up with you at some point, and before that they will simply niggle away at you. And while you're exhausting yourself by not doing them you are depriving yourself of concentrating on more interesting and exciting stuff, such as following your ambitions or simply spending time doing the things you love.

One of the premises of Feng Shui, whether you believe in it or not, is that you can't think clearly when you're surrounded by rubbish, which provides you with all the excuses you need to avoid getting on with the real life-enhancing stuff. 'I can't possibly write my novel while the flat is in such a mess!'

The message here is either ignore the mess and get on with realizing your dreams, or clear up! Do one or the other. Either option will make you feel better – as long as you stop procrastinating.

CLEARING THE DEAD WOOD

Bearing in mind the Power of Three technique (see page 21), pick three horrible jobs you've been avoiding. If you're having difficulty choosing which three then close your eyes and imagine you can instantly get rid of three tasks from your to-do list: is it clearing clutter or sorting through bills? Or writing Christmas cards or thank-you letters? It doesn't matter, they will all be done if you use the 15-Minute Rule and the Power of Three technique.

Once you've chosen your first task, decide when to start it. The first 15 minutes should be divided into 5-minute segments – the Power of Three:

First 5 minutes

What is the one thing stopping you from starting immediately? A messy desk? An urgent phone call? Desperate hunger or thirst? Deal with it now, but only within this 5-minute time slot.

Second 5 minutes

Now for the other things that might be rushing into your head screaming for attention. Jot them down in a notebook, or on your computer but NOT on a scrap of paper to deal with later. Avoid using scraps of paper – you will end up wasting so much time trying to locate them at a later date.

Third 5 minutes

Prepare anything you need that will help with the work you'll do in your next 15 minute session. Set out your special cup for tea. Don't forget, you're not going to be able to make one once you start your 15 minutes on the main task.

TACKLING THE TASK

Right, now that you've got the procrastination out of the way, you're ready to start on your chosen task. Are you ready to get going straight after the first 15 minutes? If so, great! Set your timer for the next 15-minute session and away you go. Below are some examples of how you can use the 15-Minute Rule:

Awful Admin

First 15 minutes – Brainstorm. Include everything you can think of that can help such as making three piles: Action; File; Recycle. And think of anyone who might lend a hand. You may have a friend who loves admin, who delights in organizing, who is never happier than when ploughing her way through piles of bills, papers, diary notes, telephone messages and emails. Ring her up and book her now!

When the 15 minutes are up, reward yourself with a cup of tea, a quick read, a walk or a plan to go to the cinema.

Second 15 minutes – Prioritize. You can use your 15 minutes any way you want, as long as it's productive. But if you're not quite sure where to start then prioritize. Start on the Action pile and make a deal with yourself that you will only handle each bit of paper once. It's madness the time and energy we can spend handling the same bit of paper, telling ourselves we'll 'do it later'. At the end of this task, junk or shred the Recycle pile and file what remains. Reward yourself.

Third 15 minutes – You're away now, on a roll. This time carry on as long as you want, or if you're feeling bored or fed up stop after 15 minutes, leaving it at an interesting and easy place to come back to.

Phone calls

First 15 minutes – Brainstorm. Write down all the calls you can think of that you feel you need to make. It's worth dealing with the backlog first in order to avoid wasting energy fretting about them. You might have time to start on them within your first 15 minute session. Write down: Urgent Calls, To Do Calls and the Junk ones you don't really need to make unless you have time. Again, prioritize. If you still have time in this session, make one call from the Urgent pile.

Second 15 minutes – Think about your telephone style. How much time do you waste on each call? Do you have to spend ten minutes exchanging banal pleasantries before you cut to the chase? Sometimes it's not necessary. If you want to avoid a long chat, start with a phrase like, 'Just a quick one . . . ' Be aware of how you operate and then use this second 15 minutes to make more calls from the Urgent list. When they are all ticked off, start on your To Do list.

Third 15 minutes – Proceed as before and stick to the 15 minutes if you want to. But if you feel the urge to make more calls when the session is up, by all means carry on. By now you will be beginning to experience rewarding feelings of satisfaction at having dealt with your phone call To Do list. If more calls have jumped into the arena, try to clear up as you go along. Make sure they're on the correct lists so you know you're prioritizing. When you've finished, reward yourself.

Emails

As well as paper post we often find it hard to organize our overflowing inbox. When it comes to emails, I have to confess I hoard them. When I get heart-warming ones, I want to hold on to them. And then there are all the ones I tell myself I will look at or deal with later. Not to mention the ones that could be interesting, or the ones I should take a peek at just in case I miss out on something exciting! Which is why I ended up with 700 emails in my inbox. So, if you're anything like me, here's a plan to deal with them:

First 15 minutes – Brainstorm. What is the best way for you to deal with this problem? On one end of the spectrum, some people might take a deep breath and delete the lot, which doesn't really deal with the problem because emails will continue to accumulate. On the other end, some will painstakingly go through each and every one and deal with them accordingly. Which could take some time. You do not need to be so black and white about this. Use this first 15-minute session to consider what would work for you personally but is still reasonably efficient.

Second 15 minutes – Put your plan into action. Create separate folders for the emails you seriously want to keep and start deleting the rest. Any anxiety you feel is OK, and will ease once you get started. Use the 'So what?' method of internal de-cluttering: if you lose something, so what? Is it really the end of the world? And remember that by clearing out the old you are making way for the new. Continue to use a series of 15-minute sessions to finish the job and when you're done, reward yourself!

Tricky conversations

So many of us put off tricky conversations. Be it at work or play, face to face, phone to phone, text to text, email to email, if we know it's going to be awkward we can keep putting it off until it becomes imperative that we deal with it. So, rather than wasting energy going over the same old niggles in your head, use the 15-Minute Rule.

First 15 minutes – Brainstorm. What do you want to achieve in this conversation? How do you want to feel when the conversation is over? How would you like the other person to be left feeling, even though you can't really totally control that? You are not responsible for the other person's feelings but presumably you want to know that you behaved with decency and integrity and haven't meant to upset anyone.

Second 15 minutes – Prioritize. Pick the main points that you want to make and start the conversation, preferably at a good time and not when the other person is on their way out or about to lie down with a headache. Start by saying 'Is this a good time? I would love to talk to you for a few minutes about something very important to me.' Then try to use phrases such as 'I feel', thereby taking full responsibility for your feelings rather than blaming or attacking the other person: 'I feel sad that you forgot our anniversary' is much more likely to invite a listening ear than, 'You pig! I can't believe you forgot it AGAIN!'

Third 15 minutes – Devise a plan. You may have resolved it all by now, but if not, work together to devise a plan to improve communication between you. For example, if it is an issue with your partner or best friend, you could take it in turns to listen to each other without interrupting once. Each of you will run out of steam soon enough but you will both feel really listened to. If it is a tricky conversation with a boss or colleague, ask if you can spend 15 minutes talking about the specific problem or your future working relationship and how it can be improved. Perhaps suggest regular 15-minute chats over a cup of coffee so that you can both iron out any minor problems that may have cropped up or to voice your own ideas and ambitions.

CASE STUDY: MADDY

Maddy is a psychotherapist, and this is her account of how she got to the bottom of her dreaded piles of paperwork using the 15-Minute Rule.

'Before sorting out an office full of paperwork I am wondering where on earth to start. But actually the process has started already – I'm excited about the prospect of clearing it all, yet apprehensive about letting go of the mountains of folders/paperwork that represent years of hard work and emotional investment in studying for my two degrees.

'I'm also feeling guilty about the amount of paper I am about to dispose of, but feel better knowing that I plan to recycle absolutely every page. I like the idea of all that knowledge being recycled somehow – totally illogical but it makes me feel better emotionally.'

First 15 minutes – 'I had planned to start this on Monday morning but my mum was feeling unwell so I went to see her instead. I felt frustrated because I was so keen to start but I knew that Mum had to come first. Eventually I was able to do the first 15 minutes in the afternoon but I had to squeeze it in between two other pressing commitments. Interesting that entering into this process is highlighting just how busy I am.

'I took one stack of papers from the cupboard and started to put it into three piles:
1. Read and then recycle. Am wondering when I will get the time to read this lot but I can't let it go yet, can I?

    2. Recycle immediately.

    3. Keep. Wondering where I will refile it.

'All three options provoke some anxiety. I only got one fifth of the way through the papers as I kept being distracted by interesting articles. Realize I have to be more strategic with the next 15 minutes.'

Second 15 minutes – 'I continued on the same pile of folders and papers but was more strategic this time and finished the whole pile! And eureka – I found four items I've been looking for everywhere including one particular piece of research that I've been wanting to review. A real bonus!

'I feel very pleased that I have started the de-cluttering process. I feel very positive and more motivated to carry out the next session tomorrow morning. I've planned to do 30 minutes. There's another bonus, too. When I look through the files I feel happy. Good memories come back to me when I read my lecture notes – and I remember happy times with friends and fellow students. I'm also really remembering how much I enjoyed the mental stimulation I experienced throughout my seven years of study.'

Next Morning: 30 minutes, as planned – 'It's difficult to stop at 30 minutes as I feel I am really getting a momentum going. I'm feeling less sad about letting the paperwork go and comforted by the fact that I am keeping information I want to re-read or file indefinitely. I did ten minutes over my allocated time, and became aware that not wanting to leave things undone may be a part of my personality that I should take a second look at.

'Interesting thought: Does knowing that I tend to carry on with a task until I'm done make me procrastinate more?'

Further comments – 'This is still a work in progress as I'm aware the whole house has to be de-cluttered. But it all feels a lot less overwhelming. I have been allocating 15-minute blocks of time in my diary to trawl through paperwork over the next couple of weeks. It's very important for me to do that otherwise life takes over.

'The 15-Minute Rule has now become part of life, whether it involves housework, academic work, telephone calls, etc. Now I'm off to do 15 minutes of cleaning before going to meet someone for dinner.'

Maddy hit the nail on the head when she realized that her personality trait of not wanting to leave things undone might make her more prone to procrastination. There is a part of her that's after perfection and that, as we know, is just not possible. Perfectionism stops many of us getting on with things we want to get right but don't think we have the time for!

WHEN DOING NOTHING PAYS

Feeling excited about all the good things lying ahead of you? Or exhausted at the thought of taking action? Before we go any further, let's look at the *perks* of procrastination – or what you have to gain by putting off until tomorrow what you can do today.

There are occasions when doing nothing is good. And doing nothing for 15 minutes at a time can be positively beneficial! Here are a few examples where flopping on the sofa and not lifting a finger can be extremely helpful to you:

- It helps you resist the urge to make yet another piece of toast when you're on a diet!
- Doing nothing can mean you are taking action by avoiding the telephone when you know it's too early to ring the person you had a first date with last night.
- Refusing to budge means you can't get up to go to the tobacconist or the off-licence when you've given up smoking or drinking.
- Sitting still keeps you stable when what you really want to do is chase after your retreating partner mid-argument and shout: 'And *another* thing!'

You get the picture. Doing nothing is actually taking positive action here! However, in the majority of situations, doing nothing means you are actively choosing to miss out on having a much richer and more fulfilling life.

You may want the joy of change without having to put the work in – the magic-wand syndrome. But has it happened so far? Great things may have happened to you in your life but some of the good stuff must have required some input from you.

When I quit smoking I didn't want to give it up: I wanted to have *given up*. But actively giving up seemed a huge mountain to climb. Part of me still enjoyed it, despite the smell, the fag ash, and the fear of terrible health risks associated with it. I didn't worry too much about the money side. It wasn't that I was flush but like anyone with an addiction, the expense was the least of my worries. Most of all I didn't want to go through the pain of giving up. I wanted to be able to scratch each itch as it came and not go through what I thought would be an agonizing withdrawal.

Then I thought of something that made a big difference. I wanted to want to quit! I remember thinking that if I kept repeating that to myself I might actually come to believe that I wanted to. 'I WANT TO WANT TO' I said, over and over again. I set a date for stopping and, amazingly, I stuck to it. Now if I don't want to do something that I know I should, or that is good for me, I repeat: 'I want to want to', which, along with the 15-Minute Rule, really helps me conquer procrastination.

We can all teach ourselves new ways of thinking and swap bad habits for good ones but it's when we see the benefits of change that it becomes such a rewarding experience. And of course that positively reinforces good behaviour.

I work the 15-Minute Rule into many areas of my life and the reason I do so is because it works so effectively and it brings me joy. Because the rewards are guaranteed I want to keep doing it.

Three years ago, just before I entered into a period of huge change and transformation, I remember thinking about the quote: 'If you keep on doing what you keep on doing, you'll keep on getting what you keep on getting.' I knew I didn't want that . . .

Now I look at those words from a completely different angle. If I keep up with the good stuff then good stuff will follow! And the 15-Minute Rule brings positive change and growth. That's not to say I don't slide into procrastination now and again, because I do – but I have a sure-fire tool now to get me out of it.

ACCEPT THE CHANGE

One phrase that drives me crazy is when people say gaily or smugly 'It's just the way I am.' I'm all for self-acceptance, something many of us struggle with, but that phrase is differ-ent. It's a cop-out. It's an abdication of responsibility. It's an unwillingness to change. It's usually said with a grin that is supposed to disarm you.

I remember interviewing a well-known psychotherapist and author about male anger and how to manage it.

He said: 'When a man tells me he can't control his anger I say to him, "If there were a guillotine over your penis that would fall if you didn't control your anger, do you think you would manage it?" The answer was always, without fail: "Yes!"'

We can all find ways to change if we first find the motivation.

Another screaming bugbear of mine is how some people react to the whole concept of change. 'Oh I haven't changed,' you hear them say. 'I'm the same person I always was.' And they're proud of it! How can you be proud of not moving an inch? What are they saying – that they're perfect as they are or that change is impossible? But what about growing, evolving, learning?

Before we can change anything we have to acknowledge what it is we want, or need, to change. 'Houston, we have a problem,' we have to say to ourselves. But even when the need to tackle an issue is glaringly obvious we can easily go into denial – 'I don't really have a problem.' Or, better but still unhelpful, the mañana mode: 'I'll deal with it tomorrow, next week, after Christmas, next year.' By which time your problem might have doubled in size. Procrastination can contribute to physical and emotional illness. The tension it creates can play havoc with your peace of mind, and your ability to rest or sleep and then how you feel physically. It can have a devastating effect on your relationships and your career prospects, so it really is worth 15 minutes to investigate why you do it.

I suggest sitting down with a big piece of paper and a pen and brainstorming the topic: 'Why I Procrastinate.' Write down anything that comes into your head. You should end up with a list of major reasons, minor ones, funny ha-ha ones and funny peculiar ones. Here are mine, in no particular order:

> Fear of not getting it right
> Fear of obsessing about it
> Fear of being overwhelmed by it
> Fear of opening a Pandora's Box
> Fear I should be doing something else
> Fear of change
> Fear of failure
> Fear of success

And all of this can be just about clearing up the kitchen and loading the dishwasher! Or it could just be about sorting the washing into darks, coloureds and lights!

ACTIVATE ACTION

Don't forget how important action is. And remember, you don't have to feel motivated to take action. If you master the behaviour, the thinking and feeling will catch up. Use the 15-Minute Rule to motivate yourself any time day or night.

Remember, remember, remember: you do not have to feel motivated to take action. I'm repeating this because it's such an important lesson. If you wait to feel 'in the mood' you could be waiting a very long time. But if you start, and get the wheels turning, the momentum will soon take over.

Generally speaking, if you look at a person who is highly motivated in their work you can bet your bottom dollar that they are taking lots of action in all other areas of their lives.

There's a well-known phrase, attributed to Lucille Ball: 'If you want something done, ask a busy person to do it. The more things you do, the more you can do.'

THE BENEFITS OF CHANGE

It is a fact of life that once we see the benefits of change it will be a lot easier to continue with constructive behaviour. When you know something works and you're feeling heaps better doing it, why wouldn't you believe that positive change is a good idea?

It's desperately sad to watch someone stuck in a cycle of destructive behaviour isolate themselves so that they can continue their bad habits in peace. They often feel they have no one and nothing to make good changes for, and completely discount making the change for themselves. Their self-imposed prison creates blinkers, which prevents them from seeing all around them, and limits their perspective.

It can also be deeply frustrating to watch someone who is desperately unhappy yet still resisting change.

Recently, I was talking to someone very close to me who is emerging from a time of personal trauma. She had reminded me of a beetle that had rolled over and was stuck on its back. She seemed helpless, and unable to right herself again. Then, with a little help from the 15-Minute Rule, she took the first steps to turning her life around. How utterly wonderful it is to witness someone getting back on their feet and experiencing the benefits of positive change.

'For the first time in ten years I feel excited when I wake up in the morning,' she said. 'I can now see all sorts of great possibilities ahead of me.'

She was fed up with feeling utterly miserable and decided to take action, using her 15 minutes to do three positive things: 'I prayed for help, I made an appointment with my GP and I vowed not to drink or do drugs that day,' she explained. 'And that was the beginning of my amazing recovery.'

It is worth keeping a diary of your feelings while going through a positive change in your life. Then, when you're tempted to slip back, or if indeed you do slip back to the old ways, this chart of your moods will help you remind yourself that the new approach is well worth it. Rate your feelings on a scale of 1 to 10, 1 for feeling lousy, 10 for feeling really good.

A mood chart would also be very useful BEFORE you embark on a period of positive change. Rate your feelings on a scale of 1 to 10, 1 for feeling very anxious, 10 for feeling calm and confident. It can be wonderful for you to see concrete evidence that constructive change is well worth the effort involved.

In fact, if you try the mood chart after just one 15-minute session you will see how much difference that short burst of activity will make. Copy the chart below in a notebook and whenever you use the 15-Minute Rule fill it in beforehand and again afterwards.

Mood Chart		
Analysis	Examples	Score 1-10
How I felt before deciding to make this positive change	Scared Worried Incapable Uncertain / pessimistic	
How I feel now	Pleased Confident Capable Positive	
What inspired me to make the change	A good role model This book Seeing examples of willingness / enthusiasm	
What steps have I taken to begin feeling better	Resolved to take first small step Set time aside to achieve something positive Took time to think about making a settled decision Looked for support from friends / family / therapist / counsellor	
My mood today is	Better, now that I am taking action More cheerful More positive Less stressed	

The 15-Minute Rule Chart		
Analysis	Examples	
Thoughts before setting the time	I can't do this Will this make any difference? I don't want to do this	
Feelings before setting the time	Fearful Reluctant Hopeless Depressed	Score 1-10
Thoughts after setting the time	More positive This might actually work More hopeful	
Feelings after setting the time	Less burdened Less depressed Excited (and nervous?)	Score 1-10
Thoughts after completing the 15-Minute Rule	I know I have done well to have started on this This was quite painless Surprised at how easy it was Inspired to do more Looking forward to doing more Better perspective on the remaining task(s)	
Feelings after completing the 15-Minute Rule	Elated Pleased and happy with the achievement Content Positive Hopeful	Score 1-10

Like most of us my husband, Simon, has nightmares about the piles of paperwork that scream at him in his dreams. He recently tried the 15-Minute Rule when he was trying to locate and deal with some urgent legal and insurance documents.

I asked him how he'd been feeling about the task.

'I've felt ill,' he said. 'Ill at the thought of having to do it. There's been a feeling of dread because I just haven't wanted to deal with it. I feel a weight on my shoulders and a weight on my head. If I rated my feelings on a scale of 1 to 10, where 1 is the highest level of anxiety, I'd say I was definitely at 1.'

Simon then set the timer and started on his 15-Minute Rule project. Twenty minutes later, leaving him five minutes to savour the pleasure of having carried out the 15-Minute Rule, I asked him how he was feeling.

He was very pleased. 'I feel as if a weight has been lifted,' he said. 'I have more to do but I've definitely made progress and I'm feeling much better about it. It had been haunting me all the time, every day. I will do my next 15 minutes tomorrow when I get home from work.'

And on a scale of 1 to 10 now?

'Oh a 9, definitely a 9.'

So now he's in a much happier place.

CASE STUDY: LAURA

Laura is a young, busy working woman who, over the years, has filled her wardrobe to bursting point. The problem, which on the surface seems a trivial one, was beginning to have a negative impact on her life. She wasted far too much time searching for clothes, trying to stuff them into her overflowing cupboards and even having to re-iron them because they'd become so creased.

The prospect of returning home after a hard day in the office to face the piles of clothes all over her bedroom was spoiling her enjoyment of her own home, her nice clothes and her precious free time.

Finally, Laura decided it was time for action. She applied the 15-Minute Rule to the problem and recorded her feelings throughout.

How I felt beforehand: Lousy, overwhelmed, exhausted, frustrated. I had so many clothes but nothing to wear. I could barely move in my bedroom for piles of clothes. I would try things on and if I didn't like how it looked I'd chuck it in a corner. It was a fight to get it back into the wardrobe because it was so crammed. I couldn't find 90 per cent of what I was looking for. I felt it was completely unmanageable and it was really driving me mad. Every time I walked into my bedroom my heart sank.

How I feel now: fantastic! I must have got rid of 50 per cent of my stuff yet it seems as if I have so much more to wear. I am really enjoying my clothes now. I can move around easily in my room, which has become a much more peaceful space. Another plus is that I have lots more energy. When I walk into my bedroom I feel happy, light and positive – I no longer feel worn down by the thought that I need to get to grips with my wardrobe.

What inspired me to make a change: I was feeling so miserable about the situation. Being at home depressed me. Getting ready to go to work or going out for the evening was such a chore. I was too embarrassed to invite anyone home.

Steps I've taken to feel better: I used the 15-Minute Rule. Just seconds into my first 15-minute session I was merrily sorting clothes into piles to keep, give to charity or throw in the bin (the Power of Three) and I started to feel as if a weight was easing off my shoulders. After the 15 minutes was up I knew I was well on the way to solving my problem.

My mood today on a scale of 1 to 10: It's a 10! I feel great. I should have done it years ago but I didn't know then what I know now: that just 15 minutes of action can make a whole lot of difference.

Change has a reputation for being hard. But perhaps one of the big lessons is how we perceive change: tough or easy. We see things, including problems, in many different ways. But where there is willingness the difficulties can be so much easier to overcome.

When we're tying ourselves in knots trying to look at the problem from every angle it's worth remembering this quote from Einstein:

'Any intelligent fool can make things bigger and more complex . . . It takes a touch of genius – and a lot of courage – to move in the opposite direction.'

SUMMARY

Now you know exactly how to pulverize procrastination and tackle all those horrible jobs, and that it is fear which is often behind our tendency to procrastinate. The 15-Minute Rule cuts through it all and makes you primed for action. And, better still, you will soon start to see huge benefits of constructive change.

4

WILLINGNESS AND ENTHUSIASM

'It is our attitude at the beginning of a difficult
task which, more than anything else, will affect
its successful outcome.'

William James, psychologist

Willingness and enthusiasm are two profoundly important qualities that can mean the difference between success and failure – and they work in absolute harmony with the 15-Minute Rule. Willingness is about wanting to do something; unlike willpower, which is a myth as we discovered in Chapter Two. When embarking on 15-minute sessions of whatever task you've chosen to tackle, willingness and enthusiasm are the two most helpful companions to take along for the journey.

Jumping into your 15-Minute Rule when you're raring to go is exciting and relatively easy. But if you're feeling ambivalent, then even just a little bit of willingness could get you started.

The word enthusiasm comes from the Greek *Enthousiasmos*, which means to be inspired or possessed by a divine being. Whether it's a child full of excitement describing the game she has invented or a puppy who is delighted to see you, well, you know enthusiasm when you see it!

And a lot of enthusiasm helps create momentum.

RESISTING RESISTANCE

The polar opposite of willingness is resistance: digging your heels in and refusing to budge. What a cold, lonely place that is! We've all done it. But why do we sometimes resist doing things that we know will be good for us? Doing things that can bring us happiness and fulfilment?

Is it because we are living in a society where instant gratification has become king? Is it that we want it all NOW without having to make an effort? I don't believe it's as simple as that. For example, while it may seem that fame and fortune falls easily into laps of some 'overnight success' stories, many of those who've succeeded have been willing to work for it and have attended endless rounds of auditions, practice, networking. This, coupled with their enthusiasm and positive attitudes (and talent!), has helped them achieve their goals.

So what makes some of us strive to achieve our dreams while some of us hold back? What keeps us clinging on to apathy, when we know we'd be much better off without it?

It is almost always fear, which holds so many of us back. It is usually the primary reason why people get stuck in a rut. But if you're prepared to plant a seed of willingness, however small, it could lead to wonderful things.

So how can you find willingness when there appears to be none?

What happens when we actively want to change or progress but nothing we've tried so far has helped? Often it is because we are not looking at the real source of the problem, which could be an underlying desire to keep the status quo because the change we seek is also a change we fear.

A good example of this would be someone who is unhappy in their work. They may have tried applying for other jobs, taking time off or even moving firms but when it comes to a complete career change, it seems too big a leap. Fear of failure keeps them chained to an unfulfilling career.

CASE STUDY: SUSIE

Susie had been working as a secretary for several years but always hankered after doing something else.

'The trouble was I didn't know what I wanted to do,' she said. 'Every two years I'd change companies in the hope that it would be more interesting in the next office, but it didn't seem to matter which company I worked for, I still felt unfulfilled, bored and dissatisfied.

'One day, during a long train journey, I realized I really wanted a change of direction. It felt scary because it meant I would have to give up what was safe and known to me. But I also felt a sense of relief that I'd finally made a decision to make some changes to my life.'

Not long afterwards Susie saw a television programme about training as a midwife.

'In an instant I knew midwifery was for me,' she said. 'You could say it was a gut reaction, so to speak! I rang up my best friend and she thought it sounded perfect for me.'

While the training would mean a drop in income for a while, Susie's husband was happy to support her in any way he could.

Now that she is fully trained and loving her work Susie feels her career change is one of the best decisions she's ever made.

'I wish I'd done it years ago,' she said. 'What made the difference was that I finally gave myself permission to feel the way I did and listened to my gut reaction.'

Letting go of old habits or embarking on a new lifestyle is not always easy. In fact, it's usually difficult until you've had a bit of practice. Someone once said to me: 'Think of letting go as posting a note through the letterbox. You cannot hang on to a corner of the envelope. And you cannot stick your hand in to retrieve it.'

To be willing means that you are cheerfully compliant, and open to an idea, as in someone expressing their willingness to help. The very word is evocative of a person who enthusiastically offers you a helping hand. And when someone does that, do you ask them what their qualifications are? No! Usually you say, yes, please. Or thank you very much. Which means that your willingness, with or without qualifications, will be something that helps you make the changes you wish.

Just think about the word unwilling, which conjures up a grumpy, surly, moody person, with a reluctance or aversion to helping out in any way.

Who would you rather be? Who would you rather be *with*?

So, how do you cultivate willingness?

The answer is to *commit* to change and, once again, that starts with a settled decision. Use the 15-Minute Rule and brainstorm all the reasons you want to make the big change in your life. Then use the power of positive thinking. Try the effective 'I want to want to' trick, the one I used to help me give up smoking (see page 37). If you can convince yourself you really want to get the ball rolling you will be able to conjure up the willingness and the enthusiasm will follow.

CASE STUDY: KATE

Kate wanted to clear out her daughter's bedroom. Sophie had left home two years previously and had no intention of clearing it out herself, despite Kate's pleading. She'd come to the realization that if she wanted the much-needed extra room, she'd have to do it herself.

'I really felt very unwilling to do it – I felt tight bands of pressure around my head at the moment I thought of it. I knew it would take days of my precious time and the whole project was fraught with emotion. It meant coming to terms with the fact that my daughter was fully grown and had flown the nest.

'Sophie wanted me to just leave it, saying she'd get round to it one day and part of me was in full agreement with her. But it didn't make sense as I'd just started working from home and really needed an office instead of having to use the kitchen table. I had given Sophie a year to sort out her room and, needless to say, we were still in the same situation two years later.'

Kate decided to use the 15-Minute Rule to make a start on the task.

'I was reluctant at first because I just saw days and days of clearing up ahead of me. And I was a bit angry with Sophie for not doing it herself. There were endless decisions about what to throw out and what to keep. But I was willing to spend at least 15 minutes on it, partly out of curiosity to see if the 15-Minute Rule worked and also in the hope that it might bring a little relief.'

Kate set the timer and spent the first 15 minutes brainstorming and making notes on anything that might help the problem, dealing with her emotional feelings first. Getting to grips with Sophie's room was an obvious manifestation of getting to grips with the fact that Sophie had left home – a big deal for both mother and daughter and very likely the reason why neither of them could face it. Other issues came up too – boundaries, control, choices and change.

'But at the end of that 15 minutes, having faced the fact that my emotions were preventing me from achieving something that was necessary from a practical point of view, I felt so much lighter and I was more than willing then to take the whole thing further.'

Once she began to see the benefits of change, the process became much easier. The following day Kate had a second 15-minute session.

'I couldn't wait to start! I used that time to phone Sophie and chat it through with her. We both acknowledged that we were frightened of cutting the apron strings but then after reassuring her that I would always be there for her we committed to celebrating this new stage in our lives.'

Kate and Sophie went out that very evening and talked until the early hours. 'It was so good for us. I was happy to toast her independence and she talked through her fears that I might be feeling abandoned. I could reassure her that while I missed having her around, I most definitely wasn't feeling abandoned.

'Sophie had given me full permission to steam ahead and trusted me not to throw anything away, other than obvious rubbish, until she'd seen it. I started the next 15 minutes the next morning and completely lost track of time and it was lunchtime before I looked at the clock. The room already looked so much better.'

By showing willingness to spend that initial 15 minutes on what she perceived to be an almost overwhelming task, Kate achieved her goal and today Sophie's old room is an office, complete with a sofabed for the many occasions when Sophie comes to stay.

Resistance is nothing to be frightened of and we all experience it from time to time. However, if we beat ourselves up about it, problems can creep in, because we may start to feel guilty and self-critical, which puts further obstacles in our way.

FEAR AND PROJECTION

Someone told me that Fear is an acronym for False Evidence Appearing Real. Very often our fear is related to something that belongs in the past and it also often seems to be real when it's not: whatever terrifies you now very likely has something to do with an event that is safely behind you, some trauma or unpleasant experience in your past.

So when you are feeling resistant, it really is worth asking yourself why exactly you are feeling this way. An unwillingness to trust, for example, may well have its roots in childhood and a parent who let you down badly or left you feeling that no significant adult was to be trusted. Until you acknowledge your past problems and begin to heal any wounds, you're likely to be projecting those thoughts on to everyone and everything else, thereby playing havoc with all your relationships. You may well be drawn to the familiar, even if this means surrounding yourself with people who let you down or are unable to give you what you need. But if you let go of the fear of being let down your resistance to potentially healthy relationships will diminish.

LETTING GO

I am a firm believer in accepting our thoughts, including all the unpleasant ones, and once we've accepted them, let them float away like passing clouds. The inner storms hover when we hang on to them, blowing them out of all proportion.

'It is the mark of an educated mind to be able to entertain a thought without accepting it,' said Aristotle.

The more we practise letting thoughts pass through our minds instead of engaging with each and every one of them, the easier it becomes. I wonder how practised you are at repeating past patterns? Do you tend to cling on to old ways of thinking and behaving which aren't doing you any good at all, or may even be damaging? How much effort and practice do we put into it? No wonder we've become so good at it!

Let's see how your own willingness comes into play in the following exercise:

Think of something you've wanted to do for a while but have been putting off, and then ask yourself the following three questions:

1.   Do I really want to do this?

2.   Is it fear that is stopping me?

3.   Am I prepared to put the work in?

Whether your answer to question one is yes or no, I urge you to answer the second question.

Here's my own example: I would love to speak Italian. I'll ask myself question one: Do I really want this? Answer: Yes, I would love to *speak* Italian. Whether or not I want to *learn* it is another matter. But I want to be able to gabble away in it. I think it's a beautiful language and I feel it would suit my temperament. I have made several attempts to learn using teach-yourself tapes. But the trouble is the attempts were months apart and because I worried I'd forgotten most of what

I'd learned before I had to keep going back to the beginning. Why am I not doing something I'd love to do?

We Brits are notorious for not learning languages and yet so many of us would love to at least have a working vocabulary in a language other than English. No doubt we've spent millions on tapes, CDs and signing up for courses we don't complete. How many of us actually follow through?

So, herewith question two of my experiment: Is it fear that is stopping me getting to grips with learning Italian? What is standing in my way? Here are my answers:

- Fear I won't be able to do it
- Fear I'm too old to grasp the grammar
- Fear my memory – or lack of it – will make it difficult to remember what I'm being taught
- Fear it will be hard work
- Worry that I would be better off learning Spanish
- Anxiety that I don't have the time (fear it would be a squeeze)
- What's the point in learning something I won't really need to use? (fear it would be pointless)

See how fear can slip in anywhere, even when you haven't thought about it consciously?

Now, when I look at my list, I have to wonder if I really do want to learn Italian or whether it's just a nice little fantasy.

The first question again then: Do I really want to do this? Answer: Could be yes, could be no.

The second question: Is it fear that is stopping me? Answer: All the evidence points to it!

This is why it's really worth answering the second question before you assume your answer to the first really is a definite yes or no.

When I look at my list of fears it's clear that I need to challenge my beliefs. Who says I can't do it? Me. What evidence do I have? In reality, none! In fact, when I was younger I did quite well at school with French and Latin. Am I too old to grasp the grammar? It might have been easier when I was younger but it doesn't have to be perfect, does it? What about my memory? My memory is what it is, good or not, whether or not I learn Italian. In fact learning it will probably improve it. What about the hard work? Well, it's as hard or as easy as you make it. And think how satisfying it will be. Would I be better off learning Spanish? OK, so lots of countries speak Spanish, but then lots of countries speak English too, and I still have my schoolgirl French for a few others. Anyway I want to learn Italian! Have I got the time? If I use the 15-Minute Rule, of course I can find the time. I can always start with 15 minutes a day, for a few days, and if it grabs me, I'll make more time. I am willing.

So, to repeat, my answer to the second question is yes. It is fear that has been stopping me, that's all. And the bottom line is a fear of not doing it perfectly. Perfectionism again. That old barrier that can stop us trying anything new.

I've been depriving myself of pleasure because of a misconception that it will be impossible to achieve what I desire. But now I realize that I can begin learning in a much more relaxed way and will take in what I can, and not worry about all the rest. I'm enthusiastic, and I'm bound to absorb much more of the language now that I've released the tension that goes hand in hand with perfectionism.

Now for question three: Am I prepared to put the work in? The answer is yes. I'll give it a go. Whether or not I'll stick to it, we'll see. But I'll commit to using my 15-Minute Rule on it.

ADDING ENTHUSIASM

So the willingness is there, and talking about Italian leads me very nicely back to enthusiasm. You have to admit that Italian men are an enthusiastic bunch when it comes to wooing women! Any woman, of any age, will tell you that. The Italian men enjoy flirting and put their heart and soul into it in a way an English man would find extremely difficult.

Enthusiasm is contagious! Hang around anyone who is passionate about what they are saying or doing and you cannot help but be caught up by their enthusiasm.

The combination of willingness and enthusiasm is what makes all the difference between achieving what we desire and giving up before we even get started and will propel you towards your goal.

But what if you don't have any passion for a certain task? How do you work up enthusiasm?

By taking action. And by being willing to do so, regardless of any obstructive thought that might enter your head. Imagine standing on a hilltop and releasing all the 'Yes, buts' and 'What ifs?' and all those old negative beliefs that are holding you back. Imagine embracing whatever it is you want to do and committing to a big dose of enthusiasm. Once you set the ball rolling it will soon start picking up momentum. It's not unusual to have a short burst of enthusiasm, but then to start losing interest. When you're in the gym, if you start slowing down on the exercise bike a warning signal comes up telling you to pedal faster or you will lose the programme. The beauty of the 15-Minute Rule is that when you've started your project you can either keep pedalling after 15 minutes or stop and pick up later where you left off.

Imagine yourself tackling a task with lots of willingness and enthusiasm and then imagine yourself tackling the same task without them. Think how much you'd be missing out by not embracing these two fabulous powerhouses! You have so much to lose by not grabbing them with both hands and so much to gain if you do.

To rev you up further, celebrate your willingness and enthusiasm today. Write down three projects you would like to become enthusiastic about and willing to tackle.

On a scale of 1 to 10, with 10 being excellent, 1 being not so hot, rate the willingness and enthusiasm you currently feel about each project. Look at your score, think about your attitude to each one and try reframing it. For example, instead of saying 'I haven't got the energy for it' try saying 'Energy breeds energy'. In other words, check the way you're thinking about it. If it's negative, then change it to positive.

Now think about those projects again and see if your ratings have changed.

Another essential component in the wonderful world of willingness is compassion. Please, please, throw away the stick that you beat yourself up with on a regular basis. It is useless; in fact it's a darn sight worse than useless – it seriously damages your health. If you're feeling lazy, if you can't be bothered, if you're down in the dumps or depressed, if you haven't done what you intended to, do you really think you need the stick? Of course not. What you need is an emotional boost, one that you can give yourself. Talk to yourself nicely, soothingly, telling yourself 'you'll be fine' and 'you are able to do this'. Pray if you have faith; meditate; nurture and care for yourself and feel confident that you will find the motivation – the willingness and enthusiasm – to do what you need to do.

A willingness to make changes for the better is growth. Pure and simple.

SUMMARY

Now that you are aware of the profound importance of willingness and enthusiasm why not use them in combination with the 15-Minute Rule to help you achieve your goals?

5

YOUR ACE CARD

> 'Nothing can stop the man with the right mental attitude from achieving his goal; nothing on earth can help the man with the wrong mental attitude.'
>
> Thomas Jefferson

Positive mental attitude is the key to changing your life. With the right attitude and the 15-Minute Rule there will be no stopping you from achieving your dreams.

I have created the term 'ACE card' to help you remember that Attitude Changes Everything. Try to lodge the acronym ACE firmly in your brain, because the way we perceive something influences how we deal with it. Remember the quote from Chapter Three: 'Whether you think you can or think you can't – you're right.'

From now on, when your train of thought becomes negative or damaging, remember you have that ACE up your sleeve. It is always there for you and can be used in every area of your life – your relationship with yourself and your relationships with others.

So, is there something currently troubling you? If so, how long has it been bothering you? Have you been avoiding it?

Or have you tried everything you can think of to resolve it but nothing has worked?

Why not call upon your ACE card here? Try telling yourself 'Attitude Changes Everything', and let go of the thoughts that prevent you from dealing with the issue. Try it for 15 minutes. And remember to call on willingness and enthusiasm!

With the right attitude you can tackle any problem, big or small, long-term or short-term. Try it today or try it for 15 minutes the next time you want to scream with frustration at a problem that keeps reappearing.

CASE STUDY: JANICE

'I've never been able to concentrate on anything for more than 15 minutes at a time,' said Janice, a singer/songwriter and author. 'The 15-Minute Rule has really boosted my self-esteem. Instead of spending 15 minutes in happy activity and the next two hours staring out of the window and wasting time, I felt I could break off after 15 minutes and do something else without any guilt. This meant that for the first time in my life I felt effective all day as I went from one activity to the other.

'After hearing about the 15-Minute Rule I learned a very difficult Chopin piece by playing for 15 minutes a day for four months. Sometimes I even have a 15-Minute Rule Day. This can take two forms.

'The first is that I do 15 minutes of something I don't want to do (but which needs to be done), followed by 15 minutes of something I do want to do (which is pure fun or leisure). Often if I've broken the back of an unpleasant task within the first 15 minutes, I find that I actually want to go on doing it for the next 15 minutes or longer.

'The second is where I 'play it by ear'. I let my mood dictate which activity I do first. When the timer goes off, I stop what I'm doing and ask myself what I want to do next. The answer just seems to come to me.

'After absorbing the 15-Minute Rule into my life, I have been able to apply the same approach to a whole variety of tasks, sometimes for longer periods. The important lesson I learned was to set a time limit. I have extended the principles of the Rule to enable me to set a boundary on my writing time. Now, I always take a break every sixty minutes. Once you get yourself motivated and focus on a job, and you can do that for 15 minutes at a time, it is easy to extend the period of focus and application indefinitely until it becomes an entire way of life.'

ARE YOU A HABITUAL WORRIER?

It's time to stop fretting and start living. How much energy do we waste worrying needlessly? Does it actually change anything? Do you feel that worrying about something is an insurance policy to stop something happening?

Worrying is an exhausting business and it would be good if you could first ask yourself why you are fretting so much? It may be because your parents were worriers, and you're unconsciously copying them, or because you had an insecure childhood. Maybe you've experienced a big setback that has knocked your confidence. Or maybe you just can't put your finger on a reason.

Whatever it is, worrying may have become a habit. But always be aware that habits can be broken, however great their grip.

Use the 15-Minute Rule to ride the wave of your worries. To begin with, allow yourself 15 minutes to think about the worry and mull it over. Acknowledge it. Don't try to suppress it because invariably when we try not to think about something it will pop into our heads! Then, when your 15 minutes are up, let the worry go.

Someone who helped me enormously with my own tendency to worry obsessively had three great tips that I now often use:

1. Look at the thought as if it's a passing cloud. See it and watch it pass by. Don't try to catch it and don't engage with it!
2. Imagine you're looking at a train pulling in to a station. Acknowledge the obsessive or worrying thought and decide it's a passenger you're going to put on the train. Watch it climb on board and then imagine the doors closing and the train moving off, on its way.
3. Put your obsessive worry into a mental bubble and release it into the air.

You may feel very anxious at first, but as you practise these effective methods, the anxiety will lessen. The aim here is to help you take control of your worrying habit rather than letting it control you. Use the 15-Minute Rule while following the ten-point plan below. If you're feeling in any way reluctant to try something new, then slip that ACE card out and change your attitude.

The Ten-Point Plan to Breaking the Worrying Habit

1. Replace every negative thought with a positive one. You can do this if you try. For example, imagine you have been asked to make a speech but are plagued with the thought, 'I can't speak

in public.' Now tell yourself over and over again, 'The audience will be a friendly one and I CAN speak in public.' This more positive message will mean you'll be less nervous and more confident on the big day. Remember: how we think is how we feel and if we choose to think about good things, and positive, confident thoughts, we will feel good, positive and confident.

2. Don't waste energy worrying about a problem you feel you can't immediately solve. Accept the things that are beyond your control and, again, ask yourself what you CAN do rather than what you can't. Once you've worked out whether or not you can do something about a particular problem, either try to face the problem head on or accept that there is nothing you can do and move on.

3. When fate plays a difficult hand remember that you have huge reserves of energy that will surface when you need them.

4. A good way to think about problems is to reframe them and say to yourself 'There is no problem, there is only a solution.'

5. Keep busy – action is one of the best ways to banish worry. I'm not suggesting you try to avoid your feelings, but by distracting yourself and staying active, you will stop obsessing and allow yourself time to catch your breath and get a change of perspective.

6. Put a time limit on your worries. And here is where the 15-Minute Rule comes in handy yet again.

Allow the problem a 15-minute worry time slot, and then put it aside.

7. Adopt a 'So what?' approach to life. Try to brush aside the upsets that happen to everybody and are unavoidable. If your washing machine breaks down, so what! Accept it, deal with it and move on.

8. Worry and guilt often go hand in hand. Recognize that everybody feels guilty about his or her thoughts or actions sometimes, but it is counter-productive to carry it to extremes. We all make mistakes, but having acknowledged them, and learned from them, don't keep beating yourself up. Apply the same forgiveness to yourself that you apply to others.

9. Ask yourself what worrying achieves. Very little, except fatigue and irritation. And it's so often destructive. Recognize that you may have set up a vicious circle for yourself: worrying makes you tired, and being tired makes it more difficult to keep your perspective and more likely that you will worry. Try to learn a few relaxation techniques and make sure you get enough rest to help you break the worrying habit.

10. If you've taken the steps above but find that you are still a habitual worrier, seek further help. Speak to your GP or see a specialist counsellor. Anxiety – habitual worrying – responds very well to treatment.

CHANGING YOUR ATTITUDE

If you have 15 minutes to spare, right now, or at some point during the next couple of hours, set your alarm and try the following exercise using the 15-Minute Rule:

Stop now and think about what sort of mood are you in today and why. Then write down answers to the following question:

How are you feeling?

Are you calm or anxious?

Are you cheerful or down in the dumps?

....

....

....

Rate your mood on a scale of 1 to 10, with 10 being extremely calm and 1 being extremely stressed.

Now, sit back and try to relax. Drop your shoulders – this will make you feel less tense immediately, and do some '7/11 breathing' – breathe in for the count of 7 and then out for the count of 11. Just do it for a few breaths. Now, pick up your notebook and write down the following statement:

Today I am not going to worry about anything.

I'm not referring to emergencies here, or something right in front of your nose that is demanding immediate attention. I'm talking about letting go of all the worries that are achieving nothing whatsoever – except causing you stress, tension and misery.

Now write the following statement down:

Today I am going to have a wonderful day.

You might be on a second 15-Minute segment now, and it's an extremely good investment of your time. If you write the sentences in your notebook you will be planting positive thoughts in your brain, and these thoughts can, in turn, make you feel better. Think of your brain as the most fantastic computer. Programme in the right data and all goes well – punch in rubbish and rubbish is what you will get. It's the same with our thought processes.

Wonderful days do not have to be about moons and Junes and everything going swimmingly. Although, of course, they very definitely can be. Wonderful days are those when, as Rudyard Kipling said, 'You can meet with triumph and disaster and treat those two imposters just the same.' Stuff happens – it's life – but it's how we deal with it that matters. In other words, if we adopt a good attitude, the obstacles of daily life are easier to overcome.

So now write down a third sentence:

Today I will accept with love.

Today, aim to use love to accept everything that might be tricky for you. Try to accept lovingly any fearful or stressful thoughts and feelings that might pop up, that would usually send you into a tailspin. Be kind to yourself. Parent the child within you. Comfort yourself with loving words when you have an unpleasant thought, an angry thought, an irritating thought. Love includes compassion . . . bucket loads of it if necessary.

Remember we can change how we think. For example, 'I feel so angry about this' can be restructured as 'I do feel angry about this, but I accept this thought lovingly. I'm allowed to feel angry but I refuse to react angrily towards others.' Similarly, 'I made a mistake and I hate myself for it' can become 'I am going to be compassionate and forgiving with myself. I am a human being and I need to nurture myself.'

After completing this exercise you may already be feeling better about your day, so enjoy it. Then, just before you go to bed tonight have a look at the three questions you answered earlier and rate your feelings on a scale of 1 to 10 again. If you have followed all three steps you may be feeling better, and sleeping better too.

SUMMARY

In this chapter we have looked at the power of having an ACE card – Attitude Changes Everything. If you know that you can call upon that ACE up your sleeve whenever you need it, you'll have the potential to cope with almost anything. By altering our perceptions and adopting a positive outlook, we change our approach to life and make it easier to cope with what life inevitably throws at us.

And now that you've been introduced to the secrets of the 15-Minute Rule, the following chapters will show you how to implement it in all the areas of your life.

6

WEIGHTY MATTERS

'Many of life's failures are people who did not
realize how close they were to success when they
gave up.'

Thomas Edison

In this chapter we're going to learn how the 15-Minute Rule
can help you achieve the body of your dreams, be it by losing a
few pounds or a lot more, or by generally improving the quality of your everyday diet and exercise programme so that you
feel better overall.

OUR ATTITUDE TO WEIGHT LOSS

Adopt the right attitude and the rest will follow. Don't forget
you can cope with anything for 15 minutes – even imagining
just how gorgeous you're going to look and how healthy you're
going to be! People aren't always good at being very positive
about themselves, so it's a good idea to spend some time practising doing just that! Let your imagination really go for it.

Most people diet at some time in their lives and many
women diet on and off throughout their lives; however, it's

likely that the weight will be put back on again – sometimes even more than what was lost in the first place. So, it's worth looking at how you approach weight loss and whether you see it as a short-term sacrifice or as a healthy eating plan for life. This time, armed with a new set of tools, you can be one of the minority who lose weight and then keep it off. The key is to keep up the healthy habits you develop. The aim is for those good habits to become so well and truly ingrained that they feel natural, and you won't have to think of them at all.

The 15-Minute Rule can help you use your imagination and creativity to begin healthy eating and for exercising to work for your specific needs. Start with inspiration: 'Whatever you do, or dream you can do, begin it – boldness has genius, power and magic in it. Begin it now.'

This is the Goethe quote from page 10. Copy it out and stick it in a place somewhere you'll see it several times a day.

Now pick a time, right now preferably, or at some point within the next day or so, to move on to step two: *visualize* your goal. This process is very important to helping you to get a clear picture of what you will try to achieve. And before you allow yourself to feel overwhelmed by negative thoughts, choose to banish them now. If they creep in regardless, and you start to think, 'I've tried slimming before and it never works' or 'I don't like healthy food', acknowledge them, but then try to replace the negative thought with a positive one. Think of the healthy foods you do like, and tell yourself you really can stick to your eating plan. It might be that you've lost weight before but that it has crept back on. Tell yourself that you know how to lose weight as you've managed to in the past and you can do again. But this time you're going to lose it and keep it off by adopting a different and more sustainable attitude.

Next it's step three: preparation. Make a list of the healthy meals you have enjoyed in the past, and the healthy snacks you love. If unhealthy food from your own kitchen is part of the problem, get rid of any that will tempt you and look for a healthy-eating cookbook to help inspire you and prepare to change your cooking habits. It's also worth spending some time trying to identify the habits and weak moments that have made your previous weight-loss programmes hard to stick to.

Step four is about planning. Decide when you will start your new healthy eating habits. The sooner the better (how about now?)might be the best idea but be realistic. If you are reading this on Christmas Day, or when you're just about to go out to a dinner party, tomorrow might be a more sensible choice!

Now for step five, which is implementing the 15-Minute Rule. Here are some suggestions:

- Plan your week's menu.
- Adjust your shopping list, and try to go food shopping *after* you've eaten. It's easier to resist impulse buying when you're feeling full.
- Become more aware of what you're eating and *how* you're eating. Chew slowly and savour the different flavours and textures. Avoid reading or watching television while you eat: if your mind is on other things you won't notice what you're eating, let alone how much of it.
- If you're desperate for a second helping try a bit of delayed gratification: wait 15 minutes and you may well decide you can do without. If so, congratulate yourself on resisting the unnecessary extra helping.
- If you feel the urge to snack, wait 15 minutes. Distract yourself. Again – you might find you can do without.
- Spend 15 minutes analysing that craving to eat. Ask yourself if you're really hungry or you're actually feeling stressed or bored. Eating won't deal with your feelings but acknowledging that it is these feelings that are driving you to eat may well stop you reaching for the comfort food.

CASE STUDY: JASMINE

Jasmine was fully aware that she ate for comfort but nonetheless she found it very hard to break the habit. She really wanted to lose two stone to get to her ideal weight, but she was stuck at the point where she kept losing and gaining the same 2 to 3 kilos over and over again. So, she decided to try the 15-Minute Rule. Every time she wanted to satisfy her urge to snack she would spend 15 minutes writing down what she was feeling before she put anything into her mouth.

Over the following week, she practised the 15-Minute Rule eight times and was ecstatic with the results. During that week the penny had finally dropped that food was not going to stop her feeling stressed or angry and that while the distraction of eating may have masked her feelings momentarily, the 'hangover' of feeling miserable about blowing her diet usually lasted much longer. She did succumb to her urge to snack the first couple of times but as the week progressed she felt stronger and more able to resist giving in to her cravings.

'While I'm writing out my feelings I'm dealing with them to some extent,' she said. 'And by the time the 15 minutes have passed the craving has either gone or has become much more manageable.'

After a while she found she could practise the technique without the aid of a pen and paper, by telling herself to wait 15 minutes and turning her attention to something else.

WHAT IS YOUR TARGET WEIGHT?

Before you start, you should ascertain whether your aim is to lose weight or to improve your diet in more general terms. We have become used to thinking about our weight in terms of stones and pounds, or kilograms, but we should also take notice of our Body Mass Index (BMI). BMI is used by the NHS and slimming organisations to calculate ideal weight in terms of height. It is calculated by dividing your weight in kilograms by your height in metres squared. For example, someone who weighs 100 kilograms and is 1.8 metres tall would have a BMI of 30.86 (100 divided by 3.25). There are several online websites to help you make the calculation, including *www.nhs.uk/Tools/Pages/Healthyweightcalculator.aspx*.

The National Institute for Health and Clinical Excellence (NICE) gives a range of BMI figures and what they indicate; for example, a range of 25–30 usually indicates that someone is overweight; a BMI above 30 would usually classify someone as obese. A figure below 20 would indicate that someone is underweight and a figure between 20–25 usually indicates a healthy weight. Children, adults and muscular athletes each have a different range of figures.

BMI is a guideline, not a rule, but it is usually a better marker of something to aim for than weight alone and, once you know your BMI, and if you discover you are in the healthy BMI weight range, you could still use the 15-Minute Rule to improve your diet.

Now, let's look at more ways the 15-Minute Rule can help you with weight loss. Here are four sets of 15 minutes for you to try:

First 15 minutes: Brainstorm.

Set the clock and, on a piece of paper or in a notebook, write HOW TO STAY MOTIVATED at the top of the page and then write down anything you can think of that could help you reach your goal. For example:

1. Research the most effective and healthy diets and jot down what appeals most about each of them

2. Make an appointment with my GP to discuss my diet goals

3. Set realistic targets for myself

4. Draft a list of the advantages of being a more healthy weight such as improved health, more self-confidence, etc

5. Make a list of the wonderful new clothes I'm going to buy when I reach my target weight

6. Buy a new notebook to record my progress and list tips to keep myself motivated

7. Consider pros and cons of joining a slimming club

Second 15 minutes: Start your diet.

Work out a healthy eating plan for today and the rest of this week. Look up some healthy recipes on the internet or buy a special cookbook. Make your shopping list, and substitute unhealthy foods like crisps and chocolates with healthier alternatives such as low-fat pretzels, fruit and vegetables.

Third 15 minutes: Kick-start your exercise plan.

Spend 15 minutes researching a form of physical exercise that you can manage for 15 minutes for five days a week. Most guidelines recommend five, thirty-minute sessions a week to help weight loss, but it may be more manageable for you to start with 15 minutes and work up to thirty. If you're finding it hard to motivate yourself, put your trainers on! Chances are that once you've got your kit on you'll get out for that exercise, even if it's simply a walk around the neighbourhood.

Weigh yourself, work out your BMI and take your waist, chest and hip measurements for later comparison.

Fourth 15 minutes: Start a food-and-drink diary.

Commit to listing everything that goes into your mouth and your feelings before and after you eat or drink. Your aim is to consume calories for the right reasons and not the wrong ones. Keep this up for a week. It will provide valuable information about not only *what* you're eating (you may be surprised by how many treats you allow yourself over the course of a week, for example), but *why* you are eating. Consider alternative coping strategies and healthy substitutes for the times when you are tempted to comfort eat.

We've all had days where the scales aren't saying what we'd like them to. Even if we're only a pound or two up it can play havoc with our mood – if we let it. But don't. It's so destructive. We know what happens: we feel de-motivated, we comfort eat, we feel worse and before long we're caught in a vicious circle. Using the ACE card, which we looked at in Chapter Five, will be very helpful here. Tell yourself 'Attitude Changes Everything' and put yourself back in the right frame of mind. In other words don't let 'fat' days ruin your life!

Instead, take 15 minutes to write a letter to yourself: 'Hey come on, it's only a few pounds. If you've been sticking to your diet the results will show up in a few days and if you haven't, well, don't stress, you can nip it in the bud now. You know you'll feel much better when you get back on track. Look how well you're doing. Come on, it's certainly not worth being miserable about. You deserve to be happy! Change your attitude.'

This exercise will put you in a much better position to achieve your goals as you will feel more positive about your ability to achieve them.

It doesn't really matter which diet you choose as long as it's healthy and suits you and your lifestyle. Slimming clubs are helpful for many people, who need a bit of support to make the changes easier. If you aren't convinced about joining a group, why not use your ACE card for 15 minutes to list the things that are putting you off, such as being too shy to meet new people or having to commit to a regular weekly slot. Try to change your attitude by listing the ways you could benefit from support. Would you be more motivated by a weekly weigh-in? Imagine sharing your funny diet stories with others in the same boat. Why not challenge your old way of thinking and try something new. You may be pleasantly surprised.

You could even start your own group. Just you and one friend would be all that was needed to kick it off and before long you may well have other friends and colleagues expressing an interest in joining. You could apply the 15-Minute Rule to setting it up. Spend 15 minutes compiling a list of friends who might be interested, and another 15 minutes one evening phoning round. But make sure your offer is as tactful as possible!

HOW TO KEEP IT OFF

First, believe that it is possible to maintain your new healthy weight because it certainly is. It's natural for our weight to fluctuate slightly for many reasons, such as when we give in to temptation for a special occasion, or are too busy to take our usual exercise. Stay calm and accept that slight ups and downs are normal; keeping a flexible attitude is an essential part of good mental health. The important thing is to make steady progress.

Once you reach your target it would be well worth spending 15 minutes a week on maintenance of your target weight. Keep a notebook specifically for this purpose and record your ups and downs and any helpful ideas and thoughts that have occurred to you, as these can help keep you focused. For example, write down the danger points of the week – a party, a coffee morning, etc – and work out in advance how much you can afford to indulge yourself on these occasions. Or find new exercise classes that might stop you getting in a rut with your fitness routine.

A good method of keeping an eye on your progress is to weigh yourself once a week or even just once a fortnight, without your clothes on and in the morning. Weighing yourself every day can be misleading because of various fluctuations. Whenever I feel that I've been overindulging, perhaps on a holiday when I've eaten and drank more than usual, I set aside 15 minutes to brainstorm the problem and find a solution when I return. I go through my diary to fit in an extra exercise session or two and plan the meals for a week, and by the time I'm finished I feel I am back on track.

People who struggle to control their weight are often left feeling miserable about it. But with the 15-Minute Rule you can banish that misery from your life completely.

And, finally, before you embark on any diet, I strongly recommend you discuss it with your doctor.

CASE STUDY: DIANA

Diana estimates that she has spent three weeks out of four, for years on end, feeling downhearted about her weight. She would yo-yo frequently within a ten-pound margin, taking two steps forward and two steps back. She would hop on and off the scales several times a day and then, exhausted with fretting about it, she'd give herself a week's break and eat whatever she liked without weighing herself.

When she heard about the 15-Minute Rule she was more than willing to give it a go.

She spent her first 15 minutes brainstorming the problem and getting to the bottom of her erratic eating patterns. She began to grasp the fact that she needed to make a fundamental change; otherwise, she would carry on like this indefinitely.

During her second 15 minutes she looked at new ways of approaching weight loss. She joined a slimming club that had worked for her in the past and resolved to make a commitment to consistency. She was going to stick at it until she reached her target weight.

A third 15 minutes was spent making the decision to treat herself with love and compassion and to start appreciating herself exactly as she was. She listed all her good points and acknowledged how grateful she was for how well her body worked for her. She finished by committing to let go of all the angst she felt about her weight while knowing she was on the right path to sorting it out.

Three months later Diana had reached her goal and was feeling really good about herself. Apart from the weight loss, she said she felt so much lighter in her heart.

'The 15-Minute Rule helped me get rid of all sorts of excess baggage and not just the excess pounds,' she reported happily. 'I'd learned that thinking differently allowed me to drop the weight of negative, sabotaging thoughts.'

EXERCISE

Being healthy isn't just about being a healthy weight, but also about taking regular physical exercise in order to achieve optimal fitness. If you are not a fan of the gym, or find it difficult to commit an hour or so to doing exercise, you can divide your fitness regime into bite-sized chunks. Walking briskly for 15 minutes at a time, five days a week, may feel far more manageable than gearing yourself up to go to the gym, dressing for the gym, getting there, working out for an hour or so, showering, etc. Something like walking may also keep you away from the temptation of the gym café for a large cappuccino with the 'free' biscuit on the saucer.

However, if you do like the gym, or want to persevere with it, try different machines or exercises for just 15 minutes at a time. If you've never tried something like the cross-trainers they may seem daunting at first, but devoting just 15 minutes to trying one out might lead you to discover that you like it. Ask one of the staff to help you devise a programme. For machines or activities that need less than 15 minutes, do more than one round! With a programme broken up into 15-minute slots, you can choose to complete as many as your day's schedule allows and you won't feel you are forced into an hour's workout each time you go. Anything is better than nothing.

By the way, if you haven't done any exercise for a long time and are out of shape, do check with your GP to make sure that it's safe for you. Here are two good reasons to start a sensible fitness programme:

1.   It can be fun!

We often hear that exercise is boring and it sometimes suits us to believe that it is. It's a very handy excuse if we're feeling lazy or unmotivated! But how can it be boring if it's something that makes you feel good and is so constructive? Pull that ACE from up your sleeve. Take pleasure in the feel of your body as it's working: if you're running in the park or walking, why not admire the scenery? If you're on an exercise bike, read a good book, listen to music or watch TV. Or join a class and learn to dance.

2.   There are so many rewards.

Exercise releases chemicals called endorphins into our body and these give you a feel-good boost. You'll get a great sense of achievement when you see how the exercise, in any form, helps you lose weight or tone up. You will feel more alert and energetic, it will boost your confidence and give you so much more joie de vivre!

CASE STUDY: NATHAN

As a busy accountant Nathan knew he should do more exercise but told himself he didn't have the time. In the past he had registered with a number of gyms, but gradually stopped going after a few months. His commute every day left him precious little time at either end of his day to fit in a workout.

'My trousers were beginning to get a bit tight around the waist and I felt constantly tired. I realized I really had to start doing some exercise,' he said. 'The change came when I discovered the 15-Minute Rule and used it to fit the sessions in even though my schedule was pretty manic at home and work.'

In his first 15 minutes, Nathan drew up a list of the different reasons for his lack of activity. 'I realized that being busy was an excuse, not a reason.' He then worked out realistic slots for planned activities during his weekly schedule.

He spent a second 15-minute session listing ways he could add exercise into his daily routine, such as walking to the train station or up the stairs at work, rather than taking the lift. He spent his next 15-minute session scheduling weekend runs and researching different running shoes on the Internet.

In a further 15-minute session, he leapt into action with a brisk walk around the village where he lived, getting the blood pumping and making himself feel good.

'I don't always take my full lunch hour at work but, after I had made the commitment, I began to take a 15-minute walk every lunchtime – and then extended it to a thirty-minute walk – and I felt much better for it. I progressed to running at weekends and even started setting my alarm a little earlier in the morning so I could fit in a short run before my shower.

'My trousers now fit me again and I have loads more energy.'

KEEPING YOUR MIND HEALTHY

A healthy body is a great way to keep a healthy mind. Regular exercise reduces stress, pumps oxygen around the body and makes us more alert and happier; equally, a healthy mind will help you keep your body in good shape. With a positive outlook and a feeling that you really can do what you have set out to do, you are more likely to resist the unhealthy behaviour that has prevented you from achieving your goal in the past.

You may wake up feeling off-balance, or something may happen that makes you want to throw all your good intentions out of the window. But if you are honest with yourself, you know the difference between what is good for you and what isn't. Again, trust your instinct.

Remember that instant gratification doesn't last. If you're feeling compulsive about something, and give in to it, you're not going to feel good. And giving in can lead to a downward spiral where you tell yourself: 'Oh well, I've blown it now. I might as well have that second brownie.' And so on. You'll go to bed feeling overly full and wake up feeling awful. And the chances are you'll do the same thing the following day. Until you arrest this negative thinking you will carry on allowing yourself to feel badly.

Instead, focus on the instances where you have stuck to your plan. Congratulate yourself for the fitness class you attended last night, or for resisting the chocolates your partner was scoffing. The gratification you get for doing the healthy thing will give you as much pleasure as an indulgent treat and will reinforce your determination to carry on.

EATING FOR LIFE

We need to find out what works for us as individuals and then fit it into our lifestyles accordingly. Diet and health tips are thrown at us from all angles and often contradict each other. Take the advice that is appropriate for you and then leave the rest. If one thing isn't working, try something else. Whenever you feel stuck in a groove or unmotivated use the 15-Minute Rule to brainstorm the issues that have got you to that point.

The key to weight loss is not crash diets and calorie counting but a healthy eating plan, which of course is another name for a diet. Whether you eat a lot or a little, good food or bad, you are following a diet of some description.

We know we need to eat proteins, fruit and vegetables, good carbohydrates such as brown rice and wholemeal pasta and good fats such as mono- and polyunsaturated fats that come from nuts, seeds and fish. We know that unhealthy fats such as trans-fats that come from things such as hydrogenated vegetable oils and unhealthy carbohydrates such as refined, processed foods are bad for us. But we don't always act on what we know. The trick to maintaining a healthy weight in the long-term is turning a healthy diet into a lifestyle. The 15-Minute Rule can give you the tools to do that by focusing your mind on the issue, by giving you time to plan your food intake and your exercise regime, and by helping you take action.

Good luck!

SUMMARY

In this chapter, you've seen how to use the 15-Minute Rule to help you achieve the body of your dreams, beat yo-yo dieting or simply improve your health and fitness. Remember you also have your valuable ACE card to help you turn self-sabotaging thoughts into more constructive and positive ones.

7

YOUR LOVE LIFE

'Love is something eternal; the aspect may change,
but not the essence.'

Vincent van Gogh

Whether you are happy or unhappy in a relationship or single but yearning for love, the 15-Minute Rule can help you improve your love life.

There are thousands of fabulously romantic quotes about coupledom, and of course so many of them are along the lines of Keats's 'Two souls with but a single thought, two hearts that beat as one.'

Depending on your interpretation, this could be a healthy idea, or not. If it refers to two separate people united by love, that's all well and good, but if it's about fusing two personalities into one, that's a different matter.

We can feel incredibly close to our loved ones if we're lucky, but the idea of the soulmate who totally connects on every level and fulfils all our needs is no more than a fantasy for most of us. And it's a fantasy that could stop us finding happiness in a relationship or even stop us from finding a potential partner in the first place. A good relationship involves two people who, even when they're really well suited and committed to making it work, will have problems occasionally. That's life.

Love sure makes the world go round but neediness stifles the life out of it. A relationship where one person finds it difficult to function without the other is not healthy. The happiest relationships tend to be between two people who choose to be together, rather than *need* to be together.

Even then, there is no such thing as a perfect relationship. We all have our baggage, and two sets of baggage living together takes up quite a bit of space! Often the best thing we can do, if we are experiencing problems in our relationship, or having difficulty either finding or entering into a new relationship, is to work on ourselves.

CHANGING YOURSELF

I am a Relate-trained counsellor with many years' experience and have often used a wonderful exercise called The Stones, which helps people who blame everything on the other person in the relationship.

The idea is to take a bucketful of pebbles, pick out a stone that represents you and then choose another that represents your partner. You then pick other stones to symbolize any significant others, and lay these other stones next to yours, at what you think to be the appropriate distance away. This creates a visual representation of where you see yourself in relation to others.

The picture often enables clients to access and unlock hidden emotional issues, allowing them to move forward in their relationship, and it can be very powerful and moving.

After studying the position of the various stones I would ask the client which single stone he or she would move to enable change. Those who saw their partner to blame for their troubles would pick up their partner's stone, which was usually far away from the stone representing themselves, and move it all the way over until it was sitting next to their own. In other words they required their partner to make all the movement! For some, the penny dropped right there and then. They realized, at a fundamental level, that they wanted their partner to do all the work when it came to changing. And they began to acknowledge that was unreasonable or unrealistic.

Using the 15-Minute Rule on a similar exercise could prove useful if you are going through a rocky patch in your love life. Take 15 minutes to sit alone and consider where you would see yourself in relation to your partner and where you want your partner to be. If it turns out you are expecting them to make all the changes, ask yourself whether you are being fair or realistic.

You could also try the exercise on your partner to understand how they see things. The revelation could open your eyes and help you both to find a way to meet each other halfway.

USING THE 15-MINUTE RULE TO IMPROVE YOUR RELATIONSHIP

Couples

The 15-Minute Rule can help improve and strengthen relationships and you can use it in as many ways as your imagination will let you. If you are already in a good relationship, the following section describes ways you can use the Rule to make your life together even sweeter.

Communication

Communicate, communicate, communicate! This is one of the most positive things we can do in our relationships. We know that communicating with other people, especially when they are important to us, is not always easy and at times it can be downright difficult but you can almost always communicate for 15 minutes. And if either of you are prone to flying off the handle, the time frame will help keep you focused.

You could either 'play it by ear' during your 15-minute session, just by talking and seeing what comes up, or you could set an agenda for a series of 15-minute communication sessions. I also suggest using the 15-Minute Rule for talking and listening sessions where one of you has the floor for 15 minutes to talk while the other listens without interrupting. You will then swap roles later that day or, if you're feeling too tired or emotional, the following day.

Love and Affection

Showing love and affection is hugely important but it's tricky if only one person in the relationship is demonstrative. It's worth the odd 15-minute commitment to see how best you can manage this difference. Talk to each other about what affection means to you. Discuss why you think you are the way you are when it comes to showing your feelings. For example, if you need physical signs of affection and your partner is unwilling to become a cuddler, ask him or her to show you that you're loved in other ways. And I don't necessarily mean sex! Cooking dinner for you, putting the rubbish out or just bringing you cups of tea while you are busy going through paperwork are all signs that someone cares.

Sex

The 15-Minute Rule can also work wonders for your sex life, whatever state it may be in.

Just 15 minutes of foreplay can improve sexual relationships no end!

Foreplay begins the moment you get up and it's not just about sex. It's about spending 15 minutes in the morning helping your partner get the kids ready, making a special breakfast, or paying them compliments. These are all demonstrations of love and affection. If you do the same in the evening both of you will be feeling more relaxed and less worn out when it comes to bedtime.

Invest 15 minutes a day on such matters and you could well be on your way to a healthy and satisfying sex life.

The 15-Minute Rule could help with any difficulty in your sex life, be it emotional or physical. One of the first things to flag up between you and your partner is that any issue belongs to the two of you, not just one or the other. A regular, calm discussion acknowledging this could be very helpful.

CASE STUDY: MIKE AND NANCY

Mike and Nancy suffered with the classic mismatch of sexual desire, a common predicament. Mike wanted to have sex much more frequently than Nancy (this is not just a male thing – it also happens the other way around) and it caused many arguments between them. She had reached the stage where she had gone off sex altogether and didn't dare be affectionate in case Mike misread her signals. She felt continually pestered and just wanted to retreat. Mike, on the other hand, felt more and more insecure and frustrated and started threatening Nancy by saying he might go off and find another woman. Such behaviour hardly encouraged closeness.

But they applied the 15-Minute Rule, taking it in turns to talk about their feelings in timed sessions. After five sessions, over a fortnight, they reached a compromise that was about quality rather than quantity. They decided to allocate two evenings a week for sex while on the other evenings they would just cuddle. Their sexual needs may still have been slightly out of tune but the agreement meant that

Mike didn't feel resentful or mystified at Nancy's less active libido, and Nancy felt she could show her affection with a loving hug without having to go further every night.

CASE STUDY: BOB AND LUCY

Bob and Lucy had stopped having sex and Lucy was feeling pretty hostile about it. She asked Bob if he was turned off by her and even if he had become impotent. In her mind, it was all Bob's fault. When I suggested they try the 15-Minute Rule on this problem, they readily agreed. I recommended they spend their first session on acknowledging it was a joint problem, because it affected them both.

That in itself came as a relief to them. It turned out that Bob was experiencing impotency problems but had felt too ashamed to talk about it. And so to avoid the issue, his tactic was to avoid sex altogether. Once he'd come clean about his worries, Lucy's hostility evaporated and they both felt more able to tackle the problem head on and together. Having spent that initial 15-minute session confronting the issue, they were able to move on and make an appointment to see their GP, do some research on the Internet and, importantly, commit to being open with each other about their feelings on the subject. In addition, Bob felt more relaxed and at ease – his secret had been making him feel tense and worried but he felt easier after sharing his troubles with Lucy. This also made her feel better, and had a positive effect on their love life.

Problem solving

It is much better to sort out difficult issues during the good times. When one or both of you is feeling angry or hostile it is much harder to deal with problems in a rational, unemotional way but if you're both feeling positive and are approachable you will be more open to using the 15-Minute Rule to discuss any problems you may have. And, with willingness and enthusiasm thrown in, you will be better equipped to find a solution.

CASE STUDY: EDWARD AND GINA

Edward and Gina were caught in a cycle of arguing frequently, breaking up dramatically and then having passionate reunions. This cycle had been going on for two years and the arguments centred on various different issues; however, despite everything they loved each other and wanted to make their relationship work.

I suggested they try the 15-Minute Rule to help them find the time during a happy reconciliation phase, to discuss how they could overcome their difficulties.

Their initial response was: 'Oh but we don't want to ruin the good times!'

Although it's natural to feel that way, they were ultimately convinced that it would be a good idea to talk things through when they were feeling in tune with each other. They decided to carry out three sessions of the 15-Minute Rule over a three-day period. The result? Success!

'It was so simple – we couldn't believe how easy it was,' said Gina. 'We sat down at the kitchen table for each of the sessions and in the first one we listed our grievances. When the timer went off we were actually both laughing and teasing each other and better still, laughing at ourselves.

'The second session was more serious. We both acknowledged there were real problems but also that we could do something about them if we were both willing to make changes. To my amazement Edward suggested that we go for couples counselling if we couldn't find a way through by ourselves. I was very impressed.'

The third session was spent talking about the loving and positive aspects of their relationship.

'Gina was so surprised that I had suggested couples counselling in the previous 15-minute session that she suggested we make the final 15-minute session a more positive and romantic one,' Edward said. 'I was more than happy to agree.'

Forgiveness

It would do us all a lot of good to spend the occasional 15 minutes focusing on forgiveness. Find somewhere peaceful to relax like a hot bath, or go for a walk in beautiful surroundings and devote time to thinking about forgiveness, either contemplating the subject as a whole or finding it in your heart to forgive someone who has hurt you. Or indeed forgiving yourself for mistakes that you have made, however large or small. Forgiving your partner doesn't mean you condone their behaviour. And the same applies to forgiving yourself. We might not like what we – or our partners – have done, but if there is genuine remorse and an important lesson has been learned then forgiveness is the only way forward.

Fun

Fun and laughter are very important ingredients in a relationship and humour can often be a powerful way of deflecting tension and anger. Fun also stops relationships from becoming stale. Use the 15-Minute Rule to plan some fun together such as discussing your next holiday or planning enjoyable activities to do over the next month. Again, let your imagination run free and you'll come up with all sorts of ideas. And you may find that planning them is a highly enjoyable activity in itself.

SINGLES

Why are we attracted to certain people and not others? Usually, it's down to good old chemistry. When your eyes meet across a crowded room and you feel your heart lurch it often means that you have instinctively recognized a strong, unspoken connection. Without realizing it, you've picked up on a sense of their personality, the similarities and the differences between you, and feel strongly attracted to them. When you meet someone you are attracted to, you often subconsciously hope that a partnership will strengthen your weaknesses and make you feel a stronger, more confident and happier version of yourself.

Not much to ask then, is it?!

Just to add to this potential minefield, what often attracts us, as the relationship progresses from that first meeting, is the familiar or the idealistic idea of what may make us happy, rather than what might be best for us. So, we may fall for someone who subconsciously reminds us of one of our parents, either in looks or behaviour, even if our relationship with that parent was less than ideal. We may choose someone whose early behaviour mirrors the behaviour of a previous partner, and ignore the warning signs that pointed to the failure of the previous relationship.

So, if you're looking for a relationship I strongly recommend preparing for it first. That's where the 15-Minute Rule can help.

One of the first things to be sure of is that you are indeed ready for a relationship. You may think you are raring to go, but in reality you might not be prepared to put your heart and soul into it, which means you subconsciously put difficulties in the way. There can be many reasons for this – such as hurt, grief, insecurity or fear. Whether it is the pain of an old relationship or fear of exposing yourself to a new one, acknowledging what is preventing you from meeting the right person will lift a weight off your shoulders.

Devote 15 minutes to thinking about how the past may be affecting your future, write down your thoughts if you think it would be helpful.

Maybe there's a part of you that is rejecting the very idea of a relationship? Perhaps you are frightened of being hurt or, like many others, you are suffering with feelings of low self-esteem. Some people feel they don't deserve true love, but maybe that's because they were brought up in an environment where they learned not to value or have faith in themselves.

Let this information settle for a couple of days, while you work out if there is something in your past that is preventing you from entering a relationship. After this, concentrate on the future. Spend another 15-minute session deciding if you are ready to start a relationship at the moment. Ask yourself the following questions below to help you to work this out. Try to answer yes or no before you read the comments below each question.

Question 1: Are you looking for someone to fulfil all your needs?

In reality, no one person can possibly fulfil all our needs and going into a relationship with this kind of expectation is more than likely to leave us feeling disappointed.

Question 2: Do you need your partner to make you happy?

This is a bit trickier to answer because in all honesty, if we find ourselves in a good relationship it will indeed add to our happiness. However – and it's a big however – we can't and shouldn't *rely* on other people to make us happy. We need to take responsibility for our own happiness.

Question 3: Do you feel you're 'incomplete' without a partner?

The ideal relationship is not the coming together of two halves to make one. Relationships involve two people, without one person being subsumed into the other. If both people who go into a relationship are reasonably stable emotionally, they are likely to make a very strong couple. But if either or both people are needy then it puts undue pressure on the relationship, and weakens it.

Question 4: Do you believe that all your problems will be solved by finding your perfect partner?

Another nice fantasy, but that's all it is. This is like the person who diets and thinks everything in their lives will be perfect when they reach their ideal weight. They forget that they are still the same person inside. Similarly, your ideal mate might help your problems relating to loneliness, insecurity or low self-esteem but unresolved emotional issues relating to your past will remain.

Question 5: Does the thought of giving up your independence delight you?

Again, this goes back to the desire to be one of two halves. Naturally we give up some of our independence when we begin a relationship because we have someone else to consider.

Ideally though your relationship will be equal and you'll work well when you're together but also when you are apart.

Question 6: Does the thought of giving up your independence terrify you?

If your answer is yes, why are you so frightened? Are you terrified of being suffocated emotionally? Or too scared of an emotional investment in case it goes wrong? In other words is it too nerve-wracking for you to think of putting all your eggs in one basket?

If the answer to most or all of the questions above was no, then you're well on your way to finding a partner. You're giving out the right messages and your emotional antennae are positive, warm and healthy – a big advantage if you want to be ready for the right person.

For those of you who answered yes to most of the questions above, you may have a bit more work to do in order to get into the right frame of mind to attract a partner and be ready for a relationship. The aim is to become emotionally prepared, by looking inside yourself and acknowledging your good points and working on your not-so-good points. By changing your attitude you can change how you are perceived and you may stand a better chance of attracting potential partners.

Taking the time to look at your relationship history is worthwhile and can often be very revealing. If you feel daunted at the prospect, make a commitment to spend 15 minutes on this exercise.

If your track record demonstrates an obvious pattern for picking unsuitable partners, there may well be a subconscious reason for that.

Write down the traits that represent the kind of people you are attracted to and see if these are also linked to the demise of any relationships you may have had. You may find yourself writing: 'I always choose women who I perceive to be out of my league' or 'I always go for control freaks.'

Now dig into your past to see if you can identify the root cause of your choices. Does it stem from your father's relationship with your mother? Or are you still looking to replace your first love who cruelly dumped you at school?

Knowing and understanding yourself better frees you up for positive change.

CASE STUDY: WILLIAM

William had a good job working as a roving reporter on a local paper and met many interesting people through his work; however, he had trouble forming lasting relationships. He was on a relatively low wage and still lived with his parents, despite the fact that he was in his early thirties and many of his friends were settling down with families. He professed to be desperate to find the right girl but, having been on hundreds of first dates, and with no relationship lasting longer than a few weeks, he decided to use the 15-Minute Rule to get to the bottom of his problem.

In the first 15 minutes, William noted down a few lines to describe some of the women he had dated and the reason the relationships were so short-lived, particularly when the decision not to take it further was his. He found he was writing a list of ridiculous 'flaws': 'Her accent put me off'; 'I hated her taste in music'; 'She wears terrible shoes'. When the session was over, William realized he was such a perfectionist that the tiniest 'fault' in someone else put him off immediately. He was also starting to realize that the criticisms were stumbling blocks that he'd deliberately placed to derail any potential relationship. And he identified his lack of flexibility as a desire to find a relationship as perfect as he perceived his parents' marriage to be.

In a second 15-minute session he tried to identify what had gone wrong when the rejection came from the other side. He mulled over each encounter and found that the more he liked his date, the more tongue-tied he would become and the greater the likelihood that he would say something silly or even insulting.

A further 15-minute session was spent listing the ways he could improve his chances of meeting the right girl. He resolved to work on his shyness and talk to more women in his day-to-day life, regardless of whether they were a potential date. He vowed to be less picky and to work on his perfectionist streak.

He used his final 15-minute session to research suitable dating websites.

After using the 15-Minute Rule William worked on his social skills and asked a few female friends to help him. He registered with a dating website and enlisted a female friend's help to write his profile. After a few months he met an attractive girl who shared many of his interests. His enthusiasm over the topics they had in common meant he didn't get tongue-tied which led to further, relaxed conversation.

MEETING A GOOD PARTNER

Many of us complain about our inability to meet prospective partners, but the obstacles in our way may be easily surmountable if we know exactly what they are.

Spend 15 minutes making a list of what you think may be stopping you from meeting potential partners who would be good for you. Even during that short amount of time you can gain insight into what may be going wrong. For example, you may realize that you don't make the time or effort to social-ize. It's no good sitting at home waiting for Miss or Mr Right to walk through the door; you need to make the effort. But what if you have been making an effort to socialize but you still haven't met anyone? Well, perhaps it's time to try some-thing completely different. Remember: if you keep on doing what you keep on doing, you'll keep on getting what you keep on getting.

CASE STUDY: ELLEN

Ellen, a lawyer, considered herself sociable but rarely seemed to meet single men. She had gone through a painful split from a long-term boyfriend nearly a year before, and was ready to move on. She believed that all she needed was the opportunity.

Frustrated that she wasn't meeting single men, she decided to use the 15-Minute Rule to take a closer look at what she could do better, or differently.

In her first 15-minute session, she listed the places she had been in the previous week. They included work, where there were plenty of male colleagues but none of them single; her tennis club, where she played other women; and a cinema, where she'd been to watch a film with her sister. She also had dinner at a friend's house, where she was the only single person at the table and she'd had a girls' night out, when she ended up spending the whole evening chatting to her girlfriends rather than potentially suitable men.

Her second 15-minute session was spent thinking about changing her social patterns to include going to places where she might meet the opposite sex. She rang her brother and a male friend to ask their advice.

In a third 15-minute session she rang some friends and persuaded them to go out with her to a nightclub and she researched singles' bars in the area.

In her final 15-minute session she joined a squash club, in the hope that more men played squash than tennis.

Not long after that, she met several eligible men and started dating one of them.

If you feel deep down that fear or lack of confidence are your stumbling blocks, take some time to think back to where they originated. Or perhaps you are simply shy?

If you feel your shyness is causing you difficulty, there are many effective ways to overcome it. Use the 15-Minute Rule to help you research these. Look up specialist counsellors or self-help books on building confidence, ask close friends if they struggle with shyness and, if so, how they overcome it. Look into hobbies that will help you feel good about yourself and which are therefore likely to build your self-confidence. Doing something you love, singing for example, is always enjoyable and doing it alongside people who love it as much as you makes conversation much easier to start. Join a book club, which has the benefit of providing a ready-made topic of conversation, or sign up to a dance class.

Now for the practicalities. What if you live in a remote part of the country, and you've genuinely exhausted all the possibilities of finding a local mate? In this case, you are going to need to be prepared to travel further afield or, if the situation is really getting you down, perhaps contemplate moving.

Again, use the 15-Minute Rule to brainstorm some possible solutions. For example, could you move closer to a town? Join a dating agency and widen the area that you're prepared to look in from a five-mile radius to a sixty-mile radius? Make more of an effort to visit friends who live in different towns or cities? Join groups that interest you?

Possibly you've encountered the same problem as thousands of other people; you live in a community where there are other like-minded people but you are moving in different circles. So you've got to change things. Bear in mind that you can meet a potential partner in the most unusual of circumstances but to maximize your chances, you must widen your net. Use the 15-Minute Rule to brainstorm likely or unlikely places. Don't turn your nose up at clichéd scenarios, such as salsa classes, because they often work!

One of the best ways to spur yourself into action is to use the 15-Minute Rule to sit down and make a list, however small, of activities that really interest you. And then commit to taking up at least one or two of them. Whether it's learning Italian, or kickboxing, creative writing or the guitar, you're going to enjoy it for its own sake as well as for any potential friendships that may develop as a result.

Pursuing your interests is not only constructive and creative; it is likely to give you a confidence boost. Be as sociable as you can and nurture all your friendships, because your friends can support you and introduce you to other people also.

Another option worth considering is singles' holidays or holidays that involve joining a group of other travellers, such as the kinds of organized trips that some specialist tour operators offer. Apply the 15-Minute Rule to finding a few of these companies, and then investigate. Where do they go? How many people are usually in a group? How much does it cost? Are there less expensive options? Weekend trips?

The time will fly by and you will be surprised how many

choices there are, for singles of all ages. The market is growing fast so you don't need to feel embarrassed or alone in doing this.

Apply the 15-Minute Rule to finding a reputable dating agency. For example, spend 15 minutes getting started on writing your profile, 15 minutes a day checking out potential mates, 15 minutes replying to any notes you may receive.

The very act of taking control of the situation can work wonders. A small action can be the catalyst for greater things happening, just as a pebble falling into a pond results in wider and wider ripples.

HEALING A BROKEN HEART

The pain of rejected love is undeniably awful. In fact, in saner moments, you wouldn't wish such a thing on your worst enemy! But if it's any consolation, most people will suffer at least a couple of broken hearts during their quest to find a happy and fulfilling relationship. Those who have never had to endure these agonies are either exceptionally lucky or unwilling even to tiptoe into this emotional arena.

When heartbreak happens, you can feel as if it's the end of the world. You cannot imagine you will ever get over it. He or she was *the one*, 'the love of your life' and nobody else will ever take his or her place.

And actually, that's part of the good news . . . The person you chose to love was unique, for good and for bad. You can cherish the good times and learn from the bad. To get over it, you will probably pass through all the appropriate stages of grief, including denial, anger, bargaining (for example, thinking 'I'd give anything if he/she would come back'), depression and acceptance. But, because of – or in spite of – your broken heart, circumstances will force you to move on. But what you will inevitably have learned will help you find and choose a new partner in the future.

There's no point pretending that dealing with a broken heart will be easy. The reality is that there's no way round it except through it. But please take comfort from this quote from Helen Keller: 'Often we look so long, so regretfully, upon the closed door that we fail to see the one that is opened for us.'

And the more you love, the greater your capacity for love. You may not want to hear it when you are in the depths of despair, but I promise you it's true. In the meantime, be kind to yourself, try to keep some sort of balance in your life, listening occasionally to the logical part of your brain rather than the emotional, and rest assured that as impossible as it may seem now, you *will* get over it. Let's look at how you can use the 15-Minute Rule to heal a broken heart:

FAST TRACK TO HEALING

Set some time aside to do the following exercises, daily if possible at first. You can make the session as long or as short as you like, but if you're struggling to make the time or motivate yourself use the 15-Minute Rule to get started. Make sure you make a firm commitment to start at a certain time and stick to it.

Exercise 1: De-stress your distress

Find a comfortable position, either sitting or lying down, drop your shoulders and relax. Meditate or simply close your eyes and listen to soothing music but be careful to avoid music that reminds you of your ex.

Exercise 2: Feel the pain

Avoid using alcohol, drugs, excessive shopping or anything else to dull any pain you're feeling. It doesn't make it go away; it will simply stay inside, festering. Give yourself time alone to let the pain come to the surface, admit how awful you feel and have a good cry if you want to. Then let it subside and send it on its way.

Exercise 3: Talk to someone

Try to find someone to talk to who you trust and who will be happy to listen – friends, family members, or a trained therapist or counsellor. If you're worried about boring your friends, then try to talk to a variety at different times.

Exercise 4: Seek solace elsewhere

If you believe in God, or a higher power of some kind, pray or ask for guidance and then let go. If you don't practice a religion, trust that inner voice in yourself when it tells you that you will get over this.

Exercise 5: Gratitude list

It really helps to make a gratitude list. You are likely to find there are things that you feel grateful for, despite how awful you're feeling, for example, your good friends, a great job or a supportive family. And it really does help restore perspective. You could apply the 15-Minute Rule to update and refresh your gratitude list once a week. Read it through just before you go to bed at night to end your day on a positive note.

If you are going through a painful split, or just coming out the other side, here is a structured healing plan to help you on the path of recovery, using four sets of 15-minute sessions. Taking constructive action will help you feel a little better almost immediately. You'll actively be kind to yourself and that alone will bring hope and a feeling of being nurtured.

Getting over a broken heart – the road to recovery

First 15 minutes: Brainstorm – In a notebook, write down the heading: 'What's Holding Me Back?' and then think carefully about why you feel you can't move forward. A lot of the things you write down will be common to many people in your situation, and that is a comfort in itself. For example, you may feel you were together so long that you have forgotten how to go about dating again. Or it may be that you feel unable to let go of the love you shared. What you are going through is normal, even though some things may be peculiar to you. You might be missing something about him or her that nobody else would miss. But actually that's normal too – and it's not at all unusual to miss the stuff that used to drive you mad (like making a mess while cooking for you both or taking ages to decide which DVD to rent!).

Putting your feelings down on paper will help you identify exactly what it is about that person you are missing and the fears that are stopping you from letting go of your past relationship.

Second 15 minutes: Where are you stuck? – Look at where you are in the grieving process. And yes there is a process, and it is a healing one . . . The five stages are denial, anger, bargaining, depression and acceptance. It is normal to go back and forth between these different feelings but it is easy to become stuck in one of the first four stages. Pinpoint which stage you are at and then you will know what to focus on.

Third 15 minutes: What went wrong? – Write down what went wrong in your relationship. What were the war crimes? Look at them again. Do you really want to be with someone who behaves like that? 'But I love him/her!' you might wail. Yes, but do you *like* them? Do they deserve you? Then, equally importantly, look at your part in the breakdown of the relationship. Did you behave badly? Or did you put up with nonsense and hang on in there despite your better judgement? Taking the time to look at what went wrong can help you gain valuable insights into what you are looking for from your ideal partner, work out what works and doesn't work for you in a relationship and learn from any mistakes.

Fourth 15 minutes: Fear of moving on? – Write down what you're scared of and why. Is it fear of letting go, fear of the unknown, fear of never meeting anyone again? You could go on to use a further 15-minute session to work on a care plan for yourself. This should include making sure you eat well and get enough exercise and rest. Make a list of all your current avenues of support and perhaps add some new ones, like finding a counsellor or talking to that dear old lady who seems particularly wise.

When you think about it, just four 15-minute sessions, only one hour in total, has the possibility to go a very long way towards healing a broken heart.

CASE STUDY: FELICITY

'When my ex told me he had fallen in love with somebody else, a woman he worked with, I was utterly devastated. We had been together for over two years and I had been waiting for a proposal, not a massive rejection. For the first three months I was a complete wreck, swinging from very low moods to high ones when I'd convince myself he'd realize he'd made a mistake and come rushing back to me. But then he moved in with her and I knew I had to accept the facts. My self-esteem was on the floor.

'After he'd been gone seven months I was still feeling pretty low but I knew I had to take action to pull myself out of the doldrums before I could move on, so I decided to use the 15-Minute Rule. From the moment I began the first 15-minute session I started to feel better. I saw the possibility of a happy future again.

'I spent the first session brainstorming different avenues of support, people to see and things I could do to help myself.

'During my second 15 minutes I made an appointment with my GP and then sobbed for the rest of the time. It felt good to cry but I acknowledged I was depressed. When I saw my doctor two days later we discussed whether or not antidepressants might help me and after talking about the pros and cons, I decided to give them a go.

'A third 15-minute session had me drawing up a long list of my ex-partner's faults and the things he had done to upset me. I hadn't realized there were quite so many! It was a very cathartic process which left me wondering why I had ever thought he could be 'the one'. As for my part in the break-up, well, I soon saw that I had been much too tolerant and allowed him to get away with a lot of unacceptable things like flirting outrageously with other women and standing me up when he had something better to do. I was far too easy-going. Had I challenged him more often he might have had more respect for me.

'My final 15-minute session, which I used to explore my feelings further, led to yet more insights and I came to the conclusion I was actually quite fearful – I was so frightened of being alone. I knew then that I had to really get to grips with that and soon afterwards I found a counsellor who helped me deal with my fears for the future.'

CASE STUDY: ERIC

Eric was utterly heartbroken when his girlfriend of three years walked out on him. Not only that but he hated sleeping alone in his flat. He admitted he was not coping at all well and was also in danger of losing his job as a result.

He found the 15-Minute Rule helpful, especially when he got to the fourth session, when he dealt with his fear of being alone. As a result, he decided to get himself a pet. He contacted a local cat rescue centre and within a week he had adopted a lovely ginger kitten, who soon settled in to the flat.

With an animal to look after, and company in his flat, Eric stopped feeling scared of being alone at night.

> A year later, Eric's heart fully healed, and he began dating again. And he wouldn't be without his new flatmate for anyone.

WHEN YOU DECIDE IT'S TIME TO GO YOUR SEPARATE WAYS

The 15-Minute Rule is also very helpful when you are the one who wants to end a relationship. Leaving someone can be nearly as painful as being left, more so sometimes. If you are the one who is on the receiving end then you don't really have much choice in the matter. But if you think you need to end the relationship you can drive yourself crazy beforehand by wondering if you are doing the right thing. If you have been thinking about making the break for a while but worry that you will regret it, I recommend using the 15-Minute Rule to work through all your ambivalent feelings and come to a settled decision.

Write down in a notebook all the reasons you think you want to end the relationship and, in a separate column, the thoughts that are holding you back. This will help you decide how strong your need for a break is. You will feel much more comfortable about your decision when you know exactly where you're coming from and feel confident that you've done the right thing for yourself.

Then, spend another 15-minute session working out what you want to say and the best time and place to say it.

When you have the painful meeting or, if needs be, telephone call (please don't break up by text!) then you have the 15-Minute Rule up your sleeve to help you during any overwhelming moments.

Use the examples below when the conversation becomes too emotional or angry:

- Suggest you both have a breather and talk about something else for 15 minutes.
- Go to the loo to calm down, dry your eyes if necessary and phone a friend.
- Offer your partner 15 minutes of uninterrupted listening to what he or she has to say.
- Ask him/her to listen to *you*, uninterrupted for 15 minutes while you explain why you want to end the relationship.
- If the conversation is going round in circles, switch to talking for 15 minutes about the benefits of making the break-up as amicable as possible.

SUMMARY

Shakespeare wrote that 'The course of true love never did run smooth.' But, whether you are in a relationship, coming out of one or simply looking for love, you can use the 15-Minute Rule to help you reach the next stage in your life, or enhance the relationship you are in now.

8

YOUR CAREER

'What a man can be, he must be. This need we may call self-actualization.'

Abraham Maslow, American psychologist,
who developed the theory of human motivation
referred to as Maslow's Hierarchy of Needs

I am not going to bore you with stuff you know already. This will not be a chapter offering earnest and dry career advice. Almost everything you need to help you with your career is available through the Internet and employment agencies and I credit you with the intelligence to find the resources and information yourself.

It's likely that the only thing stopping you from getting on with it is a lack of motivation. Perhaps the thought of looking for a new job is too overwhelming or you are being held back by a fear of failure. That's where the 15-Minute Rule comes in.

Few people believe they are in the perfect job but before you begin to make changes to your career you need to establish what it is you actually want. Is it a career change you're after or the same job with better perks? Are you sure you want to move at all? Use the following exercises to clarify what it is you are striving for.

ARE YOU HAPPY WHERE YOU ARE?

It's likely that you'll be able to answer this question instantly. Go with your gut reaction before thinking about it too much. Ask yourself if your situation could be better? Are you in the right place? Are you settling for less than you'd like? Are you likely to be stuck where you are for a while? Is this where you want to be?

I suggest you use the 15-Minute Rule to answer these question as honestly as you can. If there's nothing you love about your job you are obviously in the wrong place. But are you at least learning something valuable for you in the long-term? Is it giving you enough to live on?

Looking at the questions again, draw two columns – one headed 'pros' and the other headed 'cons'. List the good and bad aspects of your job. Spending 15 minutes doing this will start to clarify how you truly feel about your current situation.

If you feel like changing direction but are much too scared, it's time to stop letting fear play havoc with your self-esteem. It may feel as if you have been too cautious when you see others who have made the leap and made a success of it but it may only mean that the time isn't right for you yet to make the same move. Changes don't have to be fast by any means – slow, small steps are sometimes the better way. Instead of handing in your resignation and going back to college, for example, you could sign up for a part-time course to learn new skills. Or you could take extra courses to improve the skills you already use in your job.

NEW CAREER PLANS

If you have come to the conclusion that you are ready for a change, do you know what sort of work you'd like to do? Have you any idea? Whether you have a burning vocation, or are a bit woolly about which direction to take then try the following four sets of 15-minute sessions.

First 15 minutes: Brainstorm – This is an important task for any new project. It's fun, motivating and unleashes your creativity. In this case what would you really *like* to do? Write down what inspires you, motivates you, arouses your passion. If you're doing something you really enjoy you will put more into it and hopefully get more satisfaction in return.

Second 15 minutes: Get some support – Enlist the help of an enthusiastic friend and then run your ideas past them and see if they have any other suggestions. Ask them to help you come up with a list of all your talents, skills and strengths and discuss possible career choices with them.

Third 15 minutes: Choose your next move – Now that you have thought through and discussed various options, narrow them down to identify what it is you really want to do and work out the best route to achieving that. What are the obstacles that stand between you and your dream job? For example, if you want to become a doctor or lawyer, look into how many years of training you will need first, whether you have the qualifications to be accepted on the appropriate courses and whether you can cope financially. Perhaps instead you could consider training to be a nurse in the meantime, or a legal assistant?

Fourth fifteen minutes: Contacts – Make a list of any helpful people, agencies or organizations to approach related to your chosen career. Start drafting your cover letter and update your CV. If you need to retrain, begin the research into the courses you'll need or look into part-time courses that would fit around your current job or your family life. Search the Internet or visit your local library to find help with CVs and careers advice. If you're enthusiastic about what you are aiming for, you'll be more likely to put in the hard work.

If you need longer than 15 minutes to complete these tasks, carry on or schedule another longer session within the next three days.

'The biggest mistake people make in life is NOT making a living doing what they most enjoy,' said Malcolm Forbes, the flamboyant multi-millionaire publisher.

If you have a talent for something, and I believe everybody has a talent of some kind, then you should try to make good use of it. It is worth spending time working out how to use and develop your talents, perhaps during the brainstorming session in the previous exercise. To be in a job or career that you love brings untold rewards. Waking up in the morning really looking forward to your day, high self-esteem, a sense of purpose, creative fulfilment, happiness and good mental health, are just a few.

You may want – and possibly need – to hang on to your day job for the time being, but I urge you to give yourself a bit of a shake-up in this department to make sure you're not sitting on a potential goldmine. Sometimes striking it rich is more than making loads of money. Fulfilment is also a kind of wealth that many people wish they had.

Once you know where your talent is then try another 15-minute brainstorming session to work out whether you can use it to advance in the job you already have or to think about whether there's a job out there ideally suited to someone with your talent.

LOOK AT YOUR INFLUENCES

It's well worth using the 15-Minute Rule at least once to look at the influences that might be interfering with your career choices. Start with the parental ones because they tend to be pretty powerful. Other influences may be sibling rivalry, an overwhelming desire for safety, a desire for riches above everything else, poor teachers and peer pressure – to name just a few.

Let's consider parental influence. Even the most loving parents can steer their children, subconsciously, into unsuitable career choices. Ask yourself the following questions: are you doing what your parents wanted you to do? Are you being affected by what they said or by their choices? Are you fulfilling one parent's frustrated ambition? Or are you erring on the side of caution because they urged a life of financial security over one of risk-taking? You need to try to identify the subconscious motivations behind your choices as well as the conscious ones. Perhaps your parents' advice was driven by fear of you making the same mistakes they did? Undoubtedly, their guidance was driven by love, and wanting you to have a secure future.

Only the other day I heard about a man who was encouraging his teenage daughter to be a lawyer. 'But you did law and you hated it!' said his sister, the girl's aunt. He had bailed out of law school and clearly regretted it. So, he's asking his daughter to finish the job for him.

We also need to consider whether we are intentionally going against our parents' values or wishes when it comes to our career. How many times have we heard the children of actors saying their parents were desperate for them to have a completely different career?

Perhaps you are holding back from applying for a job because you feel you are under-qualified. These days, when it is supposed to be much more difficult to secure a good job without qualifications from school, college or university, many employers recognize that qualifications can include so much more than just exam results. Willingness and enthusiasm for something can prove just as enticing as a piece of paper to a potential employer.

Use the 15-Minute Rule to keep you motivated by devoting a set time each day to looking for and applying for jobs and using a weekly session to brainstorm any as yet uncharted avenues.

CASE STUDY: PAUL

Paul left school when he was eighteen and, although he had good A-level results, he was unsure of what he wanted to do. He loved the theatre and had gained some critical acclaim in school productions but his parents had always steered him towards university, a solid job and financial security; a safe bet when compared to a career as an actor.

He decided to take a year out and work in order to contemplate his next move and save money for university. He got a dull but well-paid desk job in London and, three years later, found himself still working for the same company and dreaming of the West End.

Frustrated, he thought he would give the 15-Minute Rule a try and sat down for his first session to brainstorm his career options. At the end of the 15 minutes he had made a firm decision to change his life and go to university.

In the second 15 minutes he began to research the various courses available and appealing to him and by the third 15 minutes he had settled on an English and drama course in Hull.

He used further 15-minute sessions to fill in the application form and send it off. And the instant that was done, he felt thrilled that he had taken a step towards a new life.

GETTING AHEAD IN THE CAREER YOU'RE IN NOW

If you feel the time is right to move ahead in your current career, how best should you go about it? It's possible that you already know, deep down, exactly what you need to do. Again, use the 15-Minute Rule to brainstorm. Write down anything that occurs to you that would help.

Then just do it! If you're already working it's worth spending time analysing what you perceive to be your current employer's strengths and weaknesses. This is, of course, after you've analysed your own first. Can you see gaps in working practice or productivity that your own talents could improve on? You might actually be able to create your own promotion and tailor-make a role for yourself within the organization you are already working for.

If there's a vacancy for an existing job that you really fancy going for, is there a little something extra you can offer? Put some time aside to think about your strengths and how you can highlight these in your interview so that they'll really be inspired to take notice of you. What makes you stand out from the rest of the contenders? A brilliant idea for the company? A skill that's unique to you?

Once you have established what you can offer, remember to add those important traits: willingness and enthusiasm. If you are passionate about the pitch you're making, this should come across naturally. If they don't, spend some time working on it. Ask a successful, confident friend to help you with a practice interview. To prepare, close your eyes, relax and think of the aspects of the job that would really excite you. Then allow yourself to believe that you'll get the job. Picture yourself working there. Where will you sit? What exactly will you be doing when you're there?

It's equally important that your new employer has an idea of your integrity and your sense of self. Give the bosses the best of yourself rather than what you think they want you to be.

If you're bending over backwards to people-please, your true talents may not be obvious.

If you are struggling to motivate yourself, or feel you are too busy to sit down and revaluate your career path, use the 15-Minute Rule to make a start.

CASE STUDY: DIANA

Diana was really fed up with her job in a large department store.

'I felt like I was on a treadmill, selling shoes every day, and I just wasn't enjoying it any more. It seemed as if the only reason I was going in to work every day was just for the pay packet at the end of the month. But I also felt stuck, and not adventurous enough to leave the company even though I really wanted a change.'

She was willing to try the 15-Minute Rule to help her choose an alternative career and find a way of achieving it. And after just four sessions – one hour – she had managed to land herself a new job.

'The first thing I did was brainstorm. I was aware of my need to feel financially secure so I acknowledged how this might restrict my choices. With this in mind, I started looking at various positions in the company I already worked for. But then I realized I didn't want to sell anything. What I really wanted was to help people. I started to think of totally new careers and I decided I wanted to work for the Human Resources department because it felt much more my sort of thing.'

Diana then used her next 15-minute session to

write down all the skills and qualities she had that she felt would be good for a job in HR.

'Because of the 15-minute time frame I didn't feel obsessive about getting it right. There wasn't time. I simply wrote down whatever occurred to me. I was actually amazed at the length of the list I had come up with. I looked down and thought, "I'd certainly employ you!" My confidence had really been boosted in just a few minutes.'

Once Diana felt sure that working in HR was the right job for her, she kept her eye on the internal jobs bulletin and within a few months, a vacancy came up. She applied and was asked for an interview. Before she went she used another 15-minute session to mull over the questions she imagined she might be asked and to think of good answers. Her interview went well and she made it on to the shortlist.

'When I was called up for the second interview I used the 15-Minute Rule to start working out just how I was going to give it my best shot. I decided there was no point trying to keep my excitement down about the possibility of a new career. And demonstrating my enthusiasm made me even keener on the job, which made me even more enthusiastic. I was so thrilled when they offered me the position just a few days later.'

Of course, it may be that you want to carry on in your current career but feel you've gone as far as you can within your company. Taking the leap and moving to a new workplace can be frightening but if you are not happy with the status quo, it's a leap you should consider taking. Use the Rule, at first, to weigh up the pros and cons. Take 15 minutes to consider the elements of your work that are stopping you from jumping ship. Are you worried about losing the security of your familiar workplace? Is the fear of leaving friends behind holding you back? Address each fear and weigh them against the potentially positive long-term effects.

When you have made your settled decision, either to stay or leave, you will be able to go forward with a clear objective. And if the conclusion is that you want to move, use regular 15-minute sessions to see what is out there and apply for the jobs that appeal to you.

GOOD WORKING RELATIONSHIPS

Even if you love your job, you may have to work with people you wouldn't choose as colleagues. Difficult working relations can have a negative impact on your life and your career, but only if you let them. The choice is yours. As prevention is better than cure, the first thing we need to look at is how to create and maintain harmony at work.

If you want to make sure you are playing your part in the smooth running of the workplace, spend 15 minutes taking a personal inventory of your relationships with your colleagues. Ask yourself the following questions, which may help you to see yourself as they do:

- Am I behaving professionally?
- Am I communicating with my colleagues on a regular basis?
- Am I respecting myself and others?
- Am I doing my job to the best of my ability?
- Am I being responsible?
- Am I willing and enthusiastic?

- Am I a good listener?
- Am I friendly and approachable?

If you find you're a bit wobbly in some of these areas, it's worth spending some time addressing them and thinking about how you could make some changes to improve your working relationships.

After you've done your personal inventory you may still think the problem is not with yourself but with a colleague. Instead of feeling cross or frustrated, resolve to work through any problems with that person. If you are struggling to find a way to broach a tricky subject, use another 15-minute session to mull it over and write down the points you want to make and the solutions that you can offer. Try to be kind, constructive and firm – you can't make changes if you're a pushover. The following questions might help:

- Is there anything I can do to make our relationship work better?
- Shall we work together on finding solutions to these problems?

Think seriously about whether you are contributing to any part of the problem. Often, when we focus on other people and any problems we might be experiencing with them, we neglect to think about what we might or might not be doing that is contributing to a difficult situation. Be honest with yourself. Is it all their fault or does a little bit of blame lie with both of you?

Apologies go a long way to alleviate a stressful situation. I'm not saying you should apologize for something that isn't your fault, but you could try saying something along the lines of, 'I'm sorry you're feeling stressed about all this. Is there anything I can do that might help?' This approach will almost certainly disarm someone who is looking for a fight.

Communicate. Talk about the feelings that surround the

problem. There's no point pretending they're not there. Taking responsibility for your feelings by using the 'I' word will often diffuse angry situations: 'I feel really upset about this' is so much more effective than, 'You've really upset me!' as saying 'I' tends to sound less accusatory and confrontational. The alternative sounds as if you are blaming the other person for making you feel that way and this will immediately put them on the defensive.

If a relationship at work breaks down to the extent that you feel you are being bullied, then you should report the matter to your line manager, department head or Human Resources department if you have one. But if things haven't gone that far then collaboration has to be the key. Suggest that both sides meet for a brainstorming session on how to begin to resolve the issue. And you know what? It could turn out to be fun. Inject humour into the meeting and you're more than halfway to finding the solution.

In short, collaborate, communicate and connect. Together, these three actions are a good way to begin resolving any kind of hostility, in any relationship.

CASE STUDY: IVAN

Ivan was a manager of an accountancy team but, despite his outgoing and confident personality, he would go out of his way to avoid confrontation; however, the behaviour of one member of the team was causing the others problems. While he was good at his job, this particular team member often behaved in an arrogant and aggressive way towards his colleagues and frequently challenged Ivan's authority, snapping at him when asked to take on a task and reacting angrily when he didn't get his own way.

Ivan began to dread telling him what to do and consequently started loading more of the unpopular tasks onto the rest of the team. When they began to resent this, Ivan knew he was making a mistake and decided he needed to tackle the problem head on. He commited to using the three 15-Minute sessions. The power of three comes up trumps again.

Session 1: Collaborate

Ivan acknowledged that he hated confrontation but accepted that he needed to bite the bullet and arrange a meeting with his difficult team member. He sent him a friendly email suggesting they have a constructive talk.

Session 2: Communicate

The meeting began with Ivan suggesting the best way to use their allocated time was to problem solve, saying that two heads were certainly better than one.

Session 3: Connect

Ivan demonstrated that he had empathy for everyone involved and was looking forward to a much more harmonious workplace for everyone. His difficult team member changed his attitude (Ivan had obviously used his ACE card) and the meeting ended with a handshake and smiles!

SUMMARY

After you've read this chapter you should be considering all the possibilities ahead of you. The 15-Minute Rule is the perfect tool to help you on your way to making the necessary changes and reaching your potential. Very few of us have to stay in a job we hate; instead, we can consider the alternatives and find a career or a job that may be more suitable. Sometimes leaving isn't the answer though; sometimes resolving and working through any issues – be it with colleagues or with the work itself – can help us rediscover enjoyment in our present career. When we're doing something we love, work can become a genuine source of joy. Being passionate about our job can bring many different rewards – financial or otherwise.

9

FINDING FINANCIAL FREEDOM

'I'm living so far beyond my income that we may
almost be said to be living apart.'

e.e. Cummings

Such witticism may raise a smile but for many people who
struggle to make ends meet the words will hit home. If you are
one of those people, this chapter is designed to help you become
free of the awful burden of financial worries. You will learn
how, using the 15-Minute Rule, you can feel much more confident and comfortable when it comes to managing your money.

First of all, what does money mean to you? Use the 15-Minute
Rule to find out. Brainstorm for 15 minutes using words, doo-
dles, illustrations, whatever comes straight from the heart.
Security? Luxury? Freedom? Poverty? Comfort? Unhappiness?
Fear? Happiness? Generosity? Meanness?

And what would you say your attitude to money is? Are you
a saver, a spender or a sensible mixture of the two? Would your
partner, friend or family agree with you?

Next, spend 15 minutes asking yourself how your emotions
are affected by money issues. Does having too little of it make
you feel anxious? Does the thought of winning the lottery make
you feel ecstatic or even relieved? We all know money doesn't

buy happiness, but having enough of it may leave you with one less thing to worry about.

No doubt we all have a few misguided ideas when it comes to our finances, many of which we picked up when we were young. It would be a very good financial investment to spend 15 minutes looking at what weird and wonderful ideas you absorbed when you were growing up. Were your parents extremely careful with money or crazy spenders? Or, as if often the case, was one thrifty while the other was generous? Did you have whatever you wanted whenever you wanted it – or were expensive treats a rarity? Did your parents argue about money? Did you, as a child, worry that there wouldn't be enough? What was your parents' attitude towards pocket money?

For my part, when I was two years old my parents split up and my mother became a single working mum to four children. It wasn't easy for her but there was always a roof over our heads and food on the table. Luxuries and holidays were a bit thin on the ground but in that generation we weren't the only ones who had to tighten our belts. I do remember my mum worrying about money and I also remember the registered letter that arrived once a week with cash from the bank. She and the bank had agreed on this plan together, doling out a set sum, to try and take control of her finances.

I have never really known what it's like to have a secure income. I didn't grow up with it and I didn't go into a job with a regular salary. When I finished my three-year journalism training I chose to go freelance. And that's how I wanted it to stay. It's been nerve-wracking at times but I wanted the freedom it gave me.

In my late twenties, after a disastrous love affair, I wasn't able to work properly because my concentration was shot to pieces and my worries began to focus on money. I told myself: 'If I can't earn, I can't survive' and I worked myself into a constant state of terror about it.

I didn't know then what I know now, which is that things don't ever stay the same. My fear was totally irrational but the feelings were horrendously real. And how can you think straight and free up energy to be creative or have fun when you're obsessively worrying about tomorrow?

Fear feeds on itself and, had I sat down and worked through my finances in a rational way, I would have been able to stop the panic by taking action.

Money terrors are awful but there is almost always a way out, especially if you use your ACE card, letting your Attitude Change Everything, and try looking at your finances from a different perspective. Organizing a budget, knowing what you can and can't spend will help to keep your worries to a minimum. If necessary, enlist the help of a friend or your bank manager. It may not be as bad as you imagine it to be, or if it is, there's always a way to manage it, little by little.

SETTING A BUDGET

You're never too old to get into this habit but the sooner you start, the better.

First 15 Minutes

Spend your first 15-minute session setting up a document on your computer or in a notebook to record your income and outgoings. We're just going to focus on your income and expenditure *today*. Forget about yesterday and don't worry about tomorrow.

Start by either setting up a new spreadsheet on your computer or by drawing two columns in your notebook. In the left-hand column, list your total monthly income (in other words the money you take home after tax, including any child benefit or other regular payments you receive). In the right-hand column, list all your regular, essential monthly outgoings such as your mortgage or rent, utilities (if you tend to get your bills every three months, divide it by three to get your monthly utilities bill), travel to work, loan or credit-card payments, and any regular direct debits or standing orders you have set up (if you're not sure what these might be, you can contact your bank and someone there will be able to tell you). Estimate an approximate monthly budget for groceries and add that figure to your right-hand column.

Income		Outgoings	
Salary / wage		Groceries	
Benefits		Mortgage / rent	
Maintenance		Loan payments	
Regular freelance income		- car	
		- personal	
		Utilities	
		- gas	
		- electricity	
		- water	
		- council tax	
		Telephone	
		- landline	
		- mobile	
		Cable / satellite TV	
		TV licence	
		Subscriptions	
		- clubs / societies	
		- magazines	
		- services	
		Insurances	
		Personal pension	
		Travel*	
Total		Total	

* If paid as a regular fixed sum, e.g. for a monthly season ticket.

Second 15 minutes

What about luxuries? It's a good idea to calculate how much you can afford to spend on luxuries or treats, which may include clothes, every month. Setting a budget doesn't mean depriving yourself of life's luxuries; instead, it means being realistic about how much you have to spend on them. If money is tight, try to identify the luxuries and any other unnecessary expenditure you could do without for a while.

Third 15 Minutes

If you've been strict with yourself and cut out any unnecessary expenditure but you're still struggling to make ends meet, try to think of other solutions. Do either you or your partner have time to fit in a part-time job? Do you really need a second car? Can you make your own lunches to take into work so that you don't have to buy them every day? A few pounds spent on a sandwich for lunch every day soon adds up to a surprising amount over a month. Can you cut down on the amount you spend on birthday and Christmas presents? Is it time to find a job that pays better? Can you cut back on holidays temporarily?

If you're lucky enough not to be struggling financially at the moment, do you save on a regular basis? If not, why not? If you have enough left over at the end of each month, instead of spending every last penny, why not make a commitment to set aside a certain amount in a separate savings account every month?

CASE STUDY: BRENDAN AND TINA

Tina and Brendan bought their first home together when they got married and took out a sizeable mortgage to do so. After the birth of their first baby,

Tina opted to give up her job as they were sure they could manage on one income. But a few unforeseen expenses, such as some essential building work, left them scraping by on the bare minimum and worried about paying their bills or what the next unexpected expenditure might be.

'We knew we couldn't go on ignoring the problem but we felt daunted at the prospect of having to face it. So we decided to use the 15-Minute Rule to deal with it and start thinking about what we could do,' said Brendan. 'We worked out how much I was earning and how much was going out, and there wasn't a lot left over.

'In a second 15-minute session, we identified a few areas where we could save – buying fewer baby clothes when we have drawers full of really good hand-me-downs, not going out for meals just because we have found a babysitter, etc. And I vowed to spend less time and money in the pub with my colleagues after work.

'In a third 15-minute session we investigated subsidized nursery places, which would free Tina up to do some part-time work. She is now working at a local florist shop a few hours a week and is thoroughly enjoying it.'

With a little extra income, and a few cutbacks, Brendan and Tina were back on track financially.

CASE STUDY: JENNY

Jenny was devastated when she lost her job. She was living alone and had a mortgage and every time she thought of the future she began to worry about finances. Friends and family tried to reassure her that all would be well, but she wasn't able to believe them; she'd gone into panic mode.

After a few weeks of fretting, but taking no action, a friend urged her to try the 15-Minute Rule. For the first 15 minutes she tried positive thinking. She lay down on her bed, breathed deeply and repeated affirmations such as 'It's all going to be OK'; 'I will get through this'; and 'I'm going to really look after myself.'

A second 15 minutes was spent brainstorming helpful and positive solutions. Instead of clinging on to the past, she decided to look to the future and see the change as an opportunity rather than a regret. She told herself: 'I can survive for a while on my redundancy pay'; 'I'm going to look for a job that I'd really like'; 'My health is good and I have a lot to be grateful for.'

Jenny's third 15 minutes was spent putting her plans into action.

'I made appointments with two recruitment agencies and looked at my bank statement online. All within 15 minutes.'

In the fourth 15-minute session, Jenny tackled her finances. 'I made a budget plan and calculated that I could eke my money out over several months by cutting back on a few things that I'd taken for granted before, like my £2.50 latte in the morning from my local café. I had an espresso maker at home and decided to start using this instead.

'Spending just 15 minutes, at four different times over three days, transformed me. I feel so much better and more positive now.'

DEMON DEBT

A male friend recently described to me 'the crushing awfulness of debt, the disaster of it all and the longing to get out of the fog'. This is a man who battled through insolvency and learned many valuable lessons along the way. Debt will never be as frightening for him again. He knows he can always play his ACE card to fend off any feelings of panic.

Use the 15-Minute Rule to get your debts into perspective:

First 15 minutes – Set the clock and start brainstorming. Write down everything that could help you, such as getting in touch with your local Citizens Advice Bureau and arranging to see them, or note down the number of Clear Start or the National Debtline. Both offer free advice. Make a list of other means of help and support that could be available to you; for example, you could go to your bank, or to a family member or friend who is good with money and whose advice you would be willing to listen to.

Second 15 minutes – Use this time to think more positively, which in turn will change the way you feel about the situation: 'There is no problem; there is only a solution.' Repeat that a few times until it sticks in your mind. By facing your debts, and finding a solution to them, you will be protecting yourself and, what's more, you will soon be in the driving seat. Next, use the remaining time to gather the paperwork you need to begin to tackle the issue.

Third 15 minutes – Now that you feel better prepared mentally, write down the amount of money you have in all your accounts, your monthly income, and the debts you are facing. Then, jot down a few ideas of your own to deal with the debts you have, such as the cutbacks that would be easiest to make.

Fourth 15 minutes – Go back to the list of trusted advisors you wrote down in your first session; for example, the Citizens Advice Bureau, your bank, a good friend – and start making those calls.

And remember that help is always at hand – you are never alone.

Debt may feel like a big mountain to climb, but if you can change your attitude towards it and stop being so frightened by it, you will feel more able to deal with it. If you have reached the point where repayments at the current level are impossible it is worth contacting your creditors to negotiate lower payments or even consider insolvency proceedings. It is important to remember that, even then, the law does offer protection to consumers in debt and advice on your legal position is available from the agencies mentioned earlier.

Whatever the outcome, burying your head in the sand and ignoring the problem is not an option. While I am not a financial expert, and I can't offer advice on stocks and shares, interest rates and mortgage deals, I have found a useful and easy way to deal with finances. And I promise you this need not take any longer than 15 minutes at a time. The aim of this exercise is to give you a clear picture of the scale of your debt and to give you ideas of how you might improve the situation.

First 15 minutes – If you haven't already done so, spend your first 15-minute session setting up a monthly budget either on your computer or in a notebook to record your regular income and outgoings (see page 127).

Just focus on your income and outgoings *today*. Forget about yesterday and don't worry about tomorrow. Set up your document with two columns and start filling them in. In the income column, enter the amount that is currently in your bank account. If it's not payday, and your bank account is empty, you've only got the outgoings column to manage. What have you spent today so far? Nothing yet? Great. You can come back later and add exactly what you've spent during the course of the day. It's a good idea to carry a little notebook around with you to record what you spend but be consistent and list everything because the idea is that you will start to see exactly where your money goes. There's no point being half-hearted about it, or only doing it when you're in the mood, because the point is to have an accurate picture of your spending.

That's all you have to do today. And then do the same tomorrow. It is so easy and will soon make you more aware of your spending habits, and make you feel more in control of your money. It's worth keeping this daily routine up even after you are firmly back in the black. The funny thing is that when something starts working for us, and we feel better, we often get a bit complacent. The pressure is off, whatever has been troubling us has passed and, if we're not careful, we can end up forgetting the lessons we've learned. And sometimes things have to get really painful again before we come to the conclusion we just might need to do something about it. With this simple daily exercise you will be able to spot potential overspending before it causes you major problems.

CHANGING YOUR FORTUNES FOR THE BETTER

As the old cliché goes, money doesn't bring happiness, but most of us have times in our lives when a little extra cash would make a big difference.

So how are you going to make that little bit extra?

I suggest you use the 15-Minute Rule to brainstorm this question, and write down anything you can think of. Sleep on it, then use the 15-Minute Rule to set your goals.

Use Step Two of my Six Stages (page 10) to help. Here's a quick summary: Visualize. Imagine yourself at your chosen goal. Feel it, taste it, touch it. Write it down.

Now for the big question: what is it you really want? If money were no object how would you be living? What effect would that have on you and your relationships? Where would you be living? What work would you be doing? Would you be unleashing your creativity?

Forget your inhibitions and fear of limitations and write it all down as if it's happening right now. You need to sense it, feel it, lodge it in your brain as if it's already happened. It will then become familiar territory and will help you achieve your goals. For example: 'I am living in a beautiful house in the country and I am in a very happy and fulfilling relationship. I am doing work that I love and I am earning enough money so that I'm not worrying about it constantly. I have a very good work-life balance so there is always time to see friends and family and have lots of fun. I wake up each morning so excited about the start of another new day. My creativity goes from strength to strength. I am healthy physically, mentally, emotionally and spiritually. I love learning new things and I really enjoy exploring the world. I am doing everything I can to make the most of my potential and I am so very grateful for all that I have.'

Read your own mission statement on a regular basis. And visualize often. Taste it, touch it, smell it . . . Then wait and see the results coming nearer and nearer to you. If you focus on what you want, and put the work in, it's very likely to happen. Dreams do come true!

THE IMPORTANCE OF TREATING YOURSELF

It may seem strange to talk about the importance of treats in a chapter on managing your finances, but I am a great believer in treats. Too much self-sacrifice makes life very dull indeed. Rewarding yourself and others is important as it reinforces a job done well and can make us all feel good. And the better you feel the more likely you are to stay focused. Rewards come in many shapes and sizes and can give us a boost when we need it. Indulge in an inexpensive treat every now again – even if it's something as simple as a hand-dipped chocolate-covered cherry from a posh chocolate shop, or a walk in the park, or going to the cinema.

Rewarding yourself for victories great and small can be a great motivator and you could use the 15-Minute Rule to design some really good ones: small, medium and large. And while we're at it, extra large as well.

A small one could be something personal that makes you feel good – such as cosmetics or toiletries, an hour chatting to an old friend or a long soak in the bath. A medium one could be a fab night out or a day off work and a large one a weekend away. As for the extra large – a fantastic holiday is always a good one. I'm not advising you to go into debt doing this – all of these rewards should be tailored to your budget and a wonderful break could mean visiting friends you haven't seen for a while.

ACE CARD WINS

Remember that the way you feel about your finances will influence your ability to deal with them. If you feel confident about your ability to manage a budget and face up to your financial responsibilities or any difficulties, you are more likely to manage them successfully. If, on the other hand, you feel overwhelmed with anxiety or have a tendency to bury your head in the sand, you are far less likely to take control.

Negative thinking can lead to financial misery. It's so important to be open to changing your attitude. Examining and identifying our attitude towards money is one of the first things we need to do to improve our lot.

There is no point worrying about money but if we strive to take control of it, rather than letting it control us, our financial situation is less likely to cause us pain.

SUMMARY

Coco Chanel once said: 'There are people who have money and people who are rich.' We can indeed be very rich with or without money and happy either way. Whatever your take on money, within this chapter you will have discovered more about your relationship with it and learned to improve how you deal with it. By using the 15-Minute Rule to take control and be proactive, money will become less of a problem for you.

10

FRIENDS AND FAMILY

'Friends are the family we choose for ourselves.'

Edna Buchanan, journalist and author

The 15-Minute Rule can work wonders with relationships, however complex. Be it family, partners or friends, 15 minutes is actually a very manageable amount of time to improve communication, demonstrate love and affection, and to resolve conflict. No relationship is perfect – we're human after all – but this chapter will help ease the way through the rough patches and help you move forward.

Communication is very important when dealing with emotionally fraught situations such as loss, separation or family rows. Talking openly with family and friends is essential in times of trouble as it not only gives them an understanding of exactly how you feel, but it will help you gain perspective on the situation yourself.

YOUR BIOLOGICAL FAMILY

Families, eh? We love them, and because we love them we

can hate them at times, too. The emotions are strong, hate is the flip side to love and where there is passion there will also sometimes be rage. Your immediate family are the people who know you best, warts and all, and they know how to make you laugh in an instant just by a look. They also know your weakness and can get under your skin just as quickly to upset you. Sometimes, too much togetherness can cause us harm.

We all know that we can't choose our biological family, our first family. If your childhood was basically happy you probably get along OK with your relatives most of the time. But if it was far from ideal, there may be ongoing issues to deal with. Every family has its spats and its fall-outs – some last five minutes, others last years; sadly, some even last a lifetime.

While there isn't always a quick fix for family conflicts, the 15-Minute Rule can be used to help you begin to resolve outstanding painful issues, improve communication and extend forgiveness to yourself and others.

Is there an incident in your family's past getting in the way of your relationship with them? Perhaps the past behaviour of a brother or sister has left you with a feeling of resentment towards them or you feel your parents took their side over yours in a row?

A family argument can stem from something as trivial as a missed birthday or as life-changing as a parents' divorce, but it almost always has its roots in the past, not the present.

Saskia's family had a major blow up when her sister Emma 'stole' her boyfriend David. 'We had been together for two years, quite happily I thought,' said Saskia, 'and then Emma threw herself at him and he dumped me for her. I was absolutely heartbroken not to mention very angry.'

Saskia vowed never to speak to Emma again and expected their parents to side with her. This was very difficult for them because obviously they loved both their daughters and while they sympathized with Saskia they didn't want to cut themselves off from Emma.

When I met them and heard the story from all sides I suggested we try the 15-Minute Rule on the situation.

Together we sat in their sitting room and each member of the family had 15 minutes to say their piece uninterrupted. Afterwards both girls understood that their parents had split loyalties and it was unfair to ask them to take sides. It was then established that the problem lay with the two sisters, old sibling rivalries – and indeed the two-timing boyfriend.

We scheduled six 15-minute sessions – one each for the three people involved, and three more with the three of them together. Communication and active listening were the main ingredients.

The conclusion was that Emma and David were actually much better suited and that Saskia had been thinking of dumping David for months! Saskia was actually growing quite fond of someone else, something that Emma knew, but David didn't, and not only was Emma feeling sorry for David but she was very attracted to him too.

Nonetheless, it was acknowledged that Saskia felt very betrayed by both of them and, thankfully, they both apologized profusely. Saskia accepted the apology and was very grateful for it. It enabled her to forgive them and move on.

ACCEPTANCE

Whatever has happened has happened. Nothing you do can change the past. But if you can accept it, rather than constantly fight against it, you are likely to feel less pain and anxiety and feel in a better position to think about what you *can* change. Hashing and re-hashing old issues and wishing things could have been different uses up huge reserves of our energy.

Instead, allow yourself to spend 15 minutes on the following exercise. Ask yourself the following questions, and any others that you come up with yourself:

1. Will the situation change if I don't accept what's happened?
2. If I choose to accept what's happened what are the consequences?
3. How will I feel if I accept what's happened?
4. Knowing what I do now, can I help myself and others go forward?

By writing down all the answers that come to mind you can begin to let go of any bitterness and improve family relations in the future. For instance, if a family member has refused to speak to you for ages, then seeing it in black and white could really help you accept what you cannot change and lead you to thinking creatively about what you can do.

SHARING THE BLAME

To an outside observer, the blame for a family rift rarely sits with one family member. But the view from within can be very different.

We can sometimes assume that most problems are caused by someone else, or, conversely, we may tend to take on the blame ourselves for everything difficult that happens. Which camp do you fall into? Again, use a 15-minute session to work out how you may have contributed to the situation. It's worth trying to take a really honest look at yourself by asking the following questions:

1. How many people were responsible for this conflict?
2. What is my part in this?

3. Should I be taking as much blame as I am?
4. How can I find a balance here?

FORGIVENESS

Being able to forgive and also to truly accept an apology is a powerful decision and can bring a great sense of release. Gandhi said, 'The weak can never forgive. Forgiveness is the attribute of the strong.' You become stronger when you choose to forgive, including choosing to forgive yourself, which is sometimes more difficult.

If this is something you struggle with, allow yourself 15 minutes to examine why. Start by asking yourself the following questions:

1. Why do I sometimes find it hard to forgive others?
2. Why do I sometimes find it hard to forgive myself for my mistakes?
3. Do I forgive others far more easily than I forgive myself?
4. Am I prepared to forgive?

Make sure your answers are honest and not just what you would like to believe. You can make a conscious effort at putting things right if you can identify the reasons why you find it difficult to forgive.

SAYING SORRY

Do you need to apologize to someone in the family? What has stopped you? Was it pride?

Or maybe you feel that you deserve an apology from someone in your family. You may end up waiting for a very long time, and with this in mind it may be worth trying to forgive them anyway. Forgiveness does not mean you condone what they've done; it just means you're going to let it go, and move on from it.

Use the 15-Minute Rule to brainstorm the reasons behind your reluctance to apologize (or to forgive) and work out what you want to do about it. Decide what you want to apologise for – was the initial act wrong or was it your reaction that blew things out of proportion? Another good use of the 15 minutes would be to write a carefully composed letter of apology if you can't bring yourself to ask for forgiveness face to face.

COMMUNICATION

There are a variety of reasons why communication between family members can be fraught: jealousy; conflict; lack of affection; fears of over-involvement in each others' lives; et cetera. If communication is something you struggle with, use a 15-minute session to think about how you might improve it. For example, if you have an awkward conversation coming up, you can spend 15 minutes thinking about what you want to say and how you wish to say it. If you find someone unresponsive, how about trying to involve someone you trust who is not emotionally involved? Family therapy can be extremely helpful as it provides a setting where both sides feel they've been listened to and when no one fears being bullied into something they don't want to agree to.

But if possible, an open, honest chat can achieve a great deal. When was the last time you really talked to a family member about something that's been bothering you? If something has been niggling at you, whether or not it's something your relative is responsible for, try to keep the lines of communication open, even if it's only by starting with a 15-minute conversation.

YOUR CHOSEN FAMILY

Our chosen family consists of our best friends. Those truly

wonderful people who we love dearly and who love us; the people you can be utterly yourself with and who love you anyway. Of course, there can occasionally be difficulties with our chosen family just as there can be with our biological one. Most of the suggestions listed above work just as well with friends as with family.

While communication can often be less of a problem with our mates, because we don't have the history and blood ties that the family network brings, problems may still arise if one of you wants to talk about something the other person would prefer to avoid. For example, if you have concerns about a close friend, it's good to try to encourage them to open up; or if it's you who is in silent mode, it's worth thinking about what you might gain by sharing your difficulties with others.

With friends, in the main, we will experience many joys, deep talks, jolly chats and hopefully lots of laughter. There will no doubt be a few tears along the way too, with betrayals, let-downs and other problems, but how wonderful it is to pick up the phone and know your closest friends will be there for you, just as you are for them. Remember, too, that not all friendships are meant to last a lifetime and sometimes run their course depending on circumstances and then come to their natural end. People sometimes grow apart when their lives take different directions. And sometimes huge differences of opinion may be non-negotiable. This is to be expected over the course of a lifetime.

DEALING WITH GRIEF

Jackie found the 15-Minute Rule both useful and supportive when the time came to sort through her mum's belongings, two years after she had died of breast cancer. Here is her story, with some extracts from her diary:

CASE STUDY: JACKIE

Jackie admitted that she kept putting off sorting her mum's things because she just couldn't face it. 'I felt sadness and guilt at getting rid of stuff Mum had treasured. But I also felt that, more than two years on, it was the right time to tackle it. I liked the idea of the 15-Minute Rule because I am very organized, and this helped me begin to sort things through, rather than half-heartedly taking things out of boxes and cupboards and then giving up and shoving them back in again!'

Day 1

'I was slow to start when I got home from work because I was feeling quite tired after my day but I realized I couldn't put it off as it would be getting dark soon, and the boxes of Mum's belongings were in my garden shed. I started by taking one box containing books out of the shed and brought the box into the sitting room. After putting it on the floor, I squatted down and started taking the books out. I sorted them into four piles: definitely keep/ not sure whether or not to keep/charity shop, sell. I was pretty focused and was so absorbed that I was quite surprised when the alarm went off at the end of the 15 minutes. I feel I've made a good start.'

Day 2

'I was actually looking forward to sorting out the remaining books today. I ended up putting some in the recycling as they were old and damaged and

I've decided to keep Dad's art books so will find somewhere suitable for them to go. I've kept quite a few of Mum's books to read and one hardback with my granny's writing in the front. I also have a huge pile for the charity shop.

'Interestingly, I felt less emotional than I thought I would. Instead I feel relieved that I've made a start on this at long last. Again, the alarm went when I wasn't expecting it. I'd finished going through another box so that was another good 15 minutes' worth of work.'

Day 3

'Today I can spend as long as I like sorting, as per the rule. My partner, Tim, went to his mother's for lunch, so I was able to sprawl out on the sitting-room floor and empty out another couple of boxes and go through them. I finished much more quickly than I thought I would and so felt really pleased with myself. Afterwards, I emailed my cousin in Australia about a letter I'd found that I thought she'd be interested in.'

Day 4

'Today I took a big box full of books to the local hospice shop. 15 minutes there and back.'

Day 5

'I really wanted to finish going through the rest of the boxes so I set aside the whole day for this alone. Although it was tiring, it was worth doing as I found some bits and pieces that I really want to hang on to and look after, such as old photos, and am English-German dictionary from the First World War, and Mum's little mirror that she used to keep in her handbag. Loads of memories came flooding back as I went through her belongings, and there were moments when I felt really sad seeing things, and remembering the happy times we had together. I also feel really glad that I've done it now and, more importantly, that I've had the chance to work out what I want to keep to remind myself of her.'

LONELINESS

In 2010 the Mental Health Foundation blamed technology and the pressures of modern life for causing feelings of loneliness among all age groups throughout Britain. Their survey of more than 2,200 adults found that one in ten people stated that they often felt lonely and one in three claimed they would like to move nearer to their family.

A study by Julianne Holt-Lunstad, a psychologist at Brigham Young University, revealed that loneliness and isolation is as bad for your health as smoking fifteen cigarettes a day or drinking too much and concludes that friendship and family can improve health by providing support during the tough times to help us find meaning in our lives. The team of researchers looked at 148 studies that tracked the relationships and health of 308,849 people over an average of seven and a half years. They found that sociable people have a 50 per cent better survival rate. The reason? 'When someone is connected to a group and feels responsibility to other people, that sense of purpose and meaning translates in to taking better care of themselves and taking fewer risks.'

In fact, GPs and health workers are now being told to take loneliness as seriously as smoking and alcoholism.

How is loneliness affecting you?

Feeling lonely is miserable at best, devastating and debilitating at worst. It can leave people feeling isolated, depressed and lethargic. And it can be a feeling that engulfs us even if we are surrounded by other people.

Being lonely is about a feeling of separateness. As we grow up there are bound to be times in our lives when we feel that sense of separateness more acutely than others. Obvious examples include when we lose somebody we love, or when we feel rejected or abandoned by a friend or loved one, or when we feel insecure. We have to learn to be alone and on our own as well as with other people. If, for example, you and your partner are experiencing problems, you may feel a sense of disconnection or isolation. Or if you've fallen out with a very close friend, or feel shut out of a particular social group, it can feel lonely, and painful.

If you feel completely overwhelmed by feelings of loneliness, confide in someone close to you or, if you feel you genuinely have no one to confide in, book an appointment to see your GP. Many people find speaking to a counsellor or therapist extremely beneficial.

LONELINESS BUSTING

If you are willing to try to change things, the 15-Minute Rule on beating loneliness can help. It's no good hoping against hope that things will magically change by themselves. So set that timer and start right now.

Acknowledging that loneliness is a problem for you is the first step to overcoming it. First, ask yourself honestly what is the root of the problem – why are you feeling lonely?

Next, ask yourself if there is anything you *can* do about and, more importantly, what you are *willing* to do about it.

Brainstorm. In a notebook, write down everything you can think of that will help you re-emerge into the world. As corny as it sounds, evening classes, pursuing new interests and hobbies, changing jobs, spending a couple of hours a week doing voluntary work, or even acquiring a pet are all tried-and-tested avenues to forming new friendships.

The great thing about being sociable is that it feeds on itself. When you extend the hand of friendship you will find more and more people who are keen to accept it. So, once you have brainstormed ideas to get yourself out and about, pick three of them, and start putting them into action. If you're a bit unsure or fearful about how to begin, start small and gradually build up. Use the 15-Minute Rule to:

Call an old friend or two and suggest meeting up.

The chances are they've been meaning to call you, too. Friendships often fall by the wayside because people intend to keep in touch and busy lives get in the way.

Write a letter or send an email.

Sending and receiving letters is rewarding in itself and the mere fact that you are connecting with someone you care about helps to banish loneliness. Write a warm and welcoming note to someone you'd love to see again. Or, if you'd prefer, write a long, chatty email to a friend you haven't seen in a long time or to someone who lives abroad.

Research a dream.

Get cracking on researching an activity that interests you. What do you enjoy? Or what new thing would you like to try? If you're not sure where to start, spend 15 minutes looking into a range of different activities, for example, drama groups, creative writing courses, dance classes, a new sport.

Write a letter to yourself.

Be your own Agony Aunt or Uncle and give yourself some sound advice. Say to yourself what you'd say to your best friend if they were in your situation.

CASE STUDY: ANNA

Anna was feeling desperately lonely when her husband's job meant they had to move from the Devonshire countryside to London. She had grown up on a farm, with acres of space all around her, and felt intimidated by the hustle and bustle and the anonymity of a big city. Her husband urged her to get a job and join a club to start meeting new people but it felt too threatening and she gradually withdrew into herself and started isolating herself.

Recognizing that things were getting worse, rather than improving, she used the 15-Minute Rule to get to the bottom of her feelings of loneliness.

To begin with, she spent one session writing to her internal Agony Aunt and another replying to herself. Writing these letters gave her the opportunity to pour out all her feelings and then, as she responded to her own letters, to come up with practical advice.

'I told myself it was good to get my emotions out but that it was time for action. I decided I would talk to my husband to explain exactly how I was feeling and then try to go out with him to meet new people together. This would help me until I felt brave enough to venture out alone. I also told myself to have patience, and not expect to make

new friends or meet new people too quickly. I also
wrote that I should give myself a pat on the back
for every achievement. I felt so much better afterwards, and I've kept the letter to reread if I need
extra encouragement.'

SEEK OUT SUPPORT GROUPS

You are not alone. If there is something specific that has made
you feel lonely – bereavement, divorce, moving house, changing jobs, redundancy, depression, motherhood, addiction or
illness – there is likely to be some sort of support group in your
area or, if not, then online. Support groups are made up of
people going through similar experiences, and so will be full of
people who know just what you're struggling with. They are an
ideal way of meeting new people, sharing ideas and receiving
emotional support. Spend 15 minutes researching local groups
in your area.

THINK THERAPY

If you're really starting to feel down and overwhelmed by feelings of loneliness, you may find it helpful to see a psychotherapist
or a trained counsellor. It can make a huge difference to your
life by providing you with a safe environment to explore your
feelings and any worries. The two biggest reasons for avoiding
professional help are lack of time and lack of money. If money
is the issue, ask your doctor to refer you to a counsellor or
psychotherapist on the NHS, or budget for fortnightly sessions
if you can't afford to see someone weekly. Some professionals
will only charge what you can afford. Prioritize your spending
if the money is, in fact, available. There is almost always a way

to find the time. Find a counsellor or psychotherapist near to your work and go in your lunch hour, or arrange evening or weekend sessions.

I've known high-earners who say they can't afford therapy and out-of-work people who say they haven't got the time. If you're using excuses to avoid counselling or therapy, use the 15-Minute Rule to look at why this might be the case. Set aside some time (as always, 15 minutes will get you started) and ask yourself the following questions:

Question: Do you think you're worth it?

Answer: You are, even if your low mood, depression or lack of self-esteem is telling you otherwise.

Question: What are you afraid of?

Answer: Many people are frightened of opening Pandora's Box, terrified of what they may have to confront. In reality, it doesn't happen like that. Your therapist or counsellor will help and support you as you discuss your thoughts, feelings and any anxieties.

Some psychologists say, 'That which we fear has already happened.' In other words, our fears for the future are often based on what has happened to us in the past. What we actually fear is the same things happening again. It's worth keeping in mind that what has happened in the past *is in the past*, not ahead of us.

We all have to deal with difficult times in our lives but things never stay the same: we get older, wiser and gain a wealth of different experiences – good and bad – to draw on to help us face the challenges ahead.

SUMMARY

Our relationships can cause us great joy or great sadness. It can be distressing to be in conflict with people, be they family or friends, who are hugely important to us. Naturally, they can have a great impact on our lives for good and for bad. In this chapter we have seen how the 15-Minute Rule can help resolve conflicts, improve existing relationships and seek out new friendships.

11

GETTING THE GLOW, INSIDE AND OUT

'The Creator has not given you a longing to do that which you have no ability to do.'

Orison Swett Marden, writer and founder of *Success* magazine

How do we nurture good physical, mental, emotional and spiritual health? I don't believe we can put these four topics into totally separate boxes. We need to look at ourselves holistically. How well are we? And how well can we become?

In this chapter we will be looking at how the 15-Minute Rule can help you achieve optimum well-being in all areas of your life.

As we have seen, how we think affects how we feel emotionally; we also need to look at the impact it has on our health. Integrating spirituality, in whatever form it takes, into our daily lives and not just putting it in a box marked 'church on Sunday', or 'good works on Saturday' can reap enormous rewards. This does not mean we have to behave perfectly every second! We are all human, and therefore flawed, but it is good to try to grow and develop and keep moving in the right direction. We will doubtless slip up and make all sorts of mistakes along the way, but if we learn from them we can be sure that we are making progress, which is what we're after, not perfection.

How many times have you heard someone say they wouldn't want to be sixteen again, or twenty-two, or thirty-five? I like hearing this because it means that person has learned some valuable lessons along the way. And what about people who proudly say they have no regrets? Certainly if I had my time again there are lots of things I would do differently but if I had done things differently I may not have been where I am today.

Life is all about balance – work with play and rest. We need to rest and recuperate on a regular basis but if you struggle to relax, it's worth devoting 15 minutes to researching new ways that might suit you personally. MIND, the mental health charity, has an excellent website with many good ideas and suggestions.

Stress-reduction courses can also help with suggestions for learning to unwind but there are other, simple techniques such as dropping your shoulders and breathing exercises that can really help reduce your stress levels. As soon as you are able to relax you start to reduce your levels of the hormone Cortisol, which is often called the stress hormone. It's earned this name because higher levels of cortisol are produced when we're in 'fight-or-flight' mode, when we are in stressful or threatening situations, and it is responsible for several stress-related changes in our bodies such as increasing our energy and sharpening our ability to think quickly. This is a good thing if we need to protect ourselves and survive but it also helps if you are put on the spot in a situation such as a high-powered board meeting. But, it's also important that our cortisol levels drop once the danger has passed so that our bodies can calm down. In modern times, the nature of the danger is more likely to be working in a stressful job than confronting a dangerous animal, and because our bodies are not always good at working out that the danger has passed we can find ourselves remaining in 'fight-or-flight' mode for long periods of time. We all know what it is like to feel stressed, and we know how important it is to 'de-stress' but many people often don't give themselves the chance to do this. Feeling permanently stressed leads to all sorts of mental health problems such as anxiety and low mood as well as physical problems such as high blood pressure.

As well as relaxation techniques, there are also many other stress-management techniques such as learning to delegate and shedding commitments. It's worth using the 15-Minute Rule to look into these if you're not sure where to start. To add to what you may know already, ask friends, do a bit of Internet research, go to the library or speak to your GP. It's important to find one or two techniques that appeal and work for you so that you have them to hand when you need them. It's also important to identify areas of your life where you can make positive changes to reduce your stress levels in the first place.

Here is a quick and very simple stress-management technique to get you started:

Sit comfortably and concentrate on your breathing. Breathe in through your nose, expanding your stomach to take in the maximum amount of air. Try not to use your shoulders – keep them still. Hold your breath for a count of six and then breathe out through your mouth. Take a couple more breaths like this and then begin to breathe normally, and in through your nose and out through your mouth. If stressful thoughts enter your mind, acknowledge them and then put them to one side. Concentrate again on your breathing and try to stay in the moment. Allow the stressful thoughts to float away as if on a passing cloud. After the first few breaths you may already feel calmer but carry on for as long as you need to. This is a technique worth repeating as you will become better at it the more you practise.

Not only are you likely to have better days if you feel less stressed, but your nights will be easier, too. If you do experience trouble sleeping, the 7/11 breathing technique described on page 66 can be very effective. If your sleeping problems persist or develop into insomnia, Cognitive Behavioural Therapy has been found to be extremely effective to help you get back to sleeping and resting normally.

Achieving a glow of well-being inside and out will leave you feeling fantastic. But the journey itself can be just as enjoyable. You will feel so much better if you know you're doing everything you can to look after yourself. None of us can always get it right, and sometimes we'll make the wrong decision, but remember: it's progress and not perfection that we're seeking.

Use the 15-Minute Rule to come up with an action plan to improve your general well-being. In a notebook draw four columns: 1. My Physical Health; 2. My Mental Health; 3. My Emotional Health; 4. My Spiritual Health. Start brainstorming ideas about how to improve your health in each of these four areas. Think of activities you know will be good for you but which you will also enjoy.

CASE STUDY: LOUIS

Louis had a stressful job and three young children and felt continually frazzled. He had no time for himself and he was tired, irritable and stressed most of the time.

After a terrible week at work, he decided to use the 15-Minute Rule to look at what changes he could make to improve his sense of well-being. He spent 15 minutes on the Friday night thinking about his mental health and what he could do to improve it. On the Saturday, he set aside two separate 15-minute sessions, one to look at his emotional health and how to improve it and the other to do the same with his physical health. On the Sunday he spent 15 minutes considering how he had neglected the spiritual side of his life and thinking about how to become more in touch with that part of himself. In the past he'd liked going to church and also enjoyed walks in the countryside where he could think about the wonderful power of nature.

By the Sunday evening he was already starting to feel much better.

'I was able to start to make some fundamental decisions that are already changing my life,' he said.

Louis made the decision to speak to his boss about cutting down on his overtime, spend more time doing fun stuff with his children, in part to give his wife a break, and have two hours every weekend to himself. 'I already feel better and less stressed because I know what changes I'm going to make. They're small things but they make me feel more in control.'

When we look after our physical, mental, emotional and spiritual lives we tend to feel better about ourselves. And when we feel better generally, we are far more likely to feel compassion, forgiveness and kindness towards ourselves which, in turn, leads to more compassion towards others. Because we are feeling good about ourselves, we are less likely to self-sabotage, making it easier to continue with the lifestyle which has been making us feel good in the first place.

ADOPTING A POSITIVE ATTITUDE

Gratitude, I feel, is an essential part of healthy living. It is the trump of your ACE card. With an attitude of gratitude it becomes easier to experience joy and to overcome the highs and lows that life throws at us.

A dear friend of mine is lying in hospital as I write this, dealing with the horrible side effects of her second series of chemotherapy. She is ten years younger than me and has three young children. Her attitude has inspired me – ever since she was diagnosed with a form of very rare cancer she has been a shining example of courage, positivity and faith. She also has willingness and enthusiasm in spades.

But she has also been terrified at times. Even so, she has not shown an ounce of self-pity and I am bursting with admiration for her partly because her attitude of gratitude is utterly inspirational: 'Since I've been ill I've had the best eighteen months of my life,' she said the other day. 'I have learned so much. I wouldn't want to swap my life with anyone else's. I accept that I am on a journey and whatever will be, will be.'

My friend accepts that she needs some conventional medical help such as chemotherapy and radiotherapy, but she now feels passionately about Qigong, a preventive and self-healing energy aspect of Chinese medicine. It consists of breathing techniques, gentle movement and meditation, which promotes healing energy. And it also encourages a sense of peace and tranquillity. She practises it regularly, and has discovered that when she can't sleep because she's so horribly uncomfortable, it also brings pain relief. Tania went into Qigong without any huge expectations. 'But from the first time I did it a light went on,' she said. 'Something clicked. It worked on every level – physical, mental, emotional and spiritual.' Even in her emotionally charged situation, she managed to find a new way of relaxing and finding peace.

I take my hat off to Tania on how well she manages to live with uncertainty, which is frightening for us all, but it's a part of life and something we all must learn to deal with.

My friend's attitude is a great example of living well within, regardless of what is happening outside your life. Her strong mental attitude helped her face tough times but it needn't be through Qigong that you turn your own negative attitude into a positive one.

LIFE BALANCE

How many of us have got the right balance between work, play and rest? Many of us swing from one thing to the next, spending too much time in one area and not enough in another, and we don't realize we're doing it until we get a nasty shock.

If you are aware that you haven't got the balance right, or if you are unsure whether you have or not, it is worth looking closely at the different areas of your life to consider how you prioritize each of them. The Wheel of Life chart, which you can download for free at *www.mindtools.com*, is a useful tool to help you do this. Either use the categories already on the Wheel of Life, or draw your own version with the following spokes: Work, Rest, Play, Spiritual Health, Partner, Family, Friends, Creativity, Health and anything else you can think of that is important to you. This tool asks you to rate each area of your life. It then gives a visual representation of how you prioritize different things in your life and this in turn will give you an idea of which areas need attention. This exercise only takes a few minutes, so why not apply the 15-Minute Rule and use the remaining time to think about how to make changes in any areas that you feel need it.

Georgie, in the case study below, tried this exercise and it helped her realize that two key areas she was neglecting were partner and family. She decided to prioritize meeting someone after being single for three years. She longed to meet that special person and have children before it was too late. She decided to use the 15-Minute Rule to help things along a bit.

CASE STUDY: GEORGIE

'My first 15 minutes was spent considering what I really wanted in a partner. I realized that good looks and money would be very nice but were far from essential. What was important to me was intelligence, a sense of humour, integrity and being with someone I could trust.

'During my next 15-minute session, I wrote down what I felt I had to offer in a relationship. When I got stuck after three things, I asked a trusted friend what they thought were my best attributes and I ended up with about two dozen! This exercise had a huge effect on my confidence and self-esteem.

'My third session was spent brainstorming possible ways to meet a new partner. I thought I'd tried all possible avenues in the past so I couldn't believe how many ideas I'd come up with. I allowed myself to be as creative as possible and apart from the obvious things like internet dating and joining a gym or a tennis club I found I'd put, "Draw up a list of everyone I know in a relationship and ask where they met their partner" and "Brave a singles holiday". I also put "Talk to that gorgeous man who smiles at me on the train every morning!" After I carried out these exercises, I felt much more aware of what I am looking for and positive about what I have to offer and how I'm going to go about meeting someone new. I feel excited about what's around the corner. I have actually started going out on dates and I have met a couple of interesting guys. Watch this space!'

THE IMPORTANCE OF FUN

This chapter is all about well-being so it's important to remember the adage, 'Laughter is the best medicine.' There's nothing quite like a good old belly laugh to leave you feeling de-stressed.

As William Arthur Ward, author of *Fountains of Faith*, said: 'A well-developed sense of humour is the pole that adds balance to your step as you walk the tightrope of life.'

Humour is essential to life. What a difference it makes! I knew someone who couldn't help laughing at funerals and crying at weddings. I guess it was his attempt to find a balance. Fun means you are able to play, to laugh, to let your hair down, to be spontaneous and to revel in a sense of joie de vivre. From time to time you may feel as if you've lost the ability to let go, in which case, it's a good idea to team up with somebody who will remind you how.

But first, you have to be *willing* to have fun!

If you're feeling unwilling to have a little fun or just feeling uninspired, use the 15-Minute Rule to brainstorm how having more fun might improve your well-being. Spend the time thinking about different kinds of activities that might be enjoyable. An outing with an amusing friend? A night on the sofa with a close friend and a box-set of your favourite comedy? An adventure, such as getting on a train to somewhere you've never been before? A trip to an amusement park? Be your own best friend and give yourself advice about what could be good fun for you today.

If you're struggling, get out your ACE card. Remember: Attitude Changes Everything. Determine to inject more fun into your life.

CASE STUDY: ROB

Rob is an IT manager who is married with three children. He is someone who feels he's not a naturally fun-loving man but when pushed he does admit he needs more pleasure and enjoyment in his life.

'I don't put fun in my hierarchy of needs,' he said. 'I burden myself with other weightier responsibilities. I'm a serious person. I was a serious little boy – people remarked on it. It is who I am.'

I asked Rob to sit down with me for 15 minutes to explore the issue and within seconds he came to the conclusion that there is a need to have fun and laughter! 'It would be a healthy counter balance to my responsibilities. And it would be a stress reliever. '

I pointed out the dangers of labelling oneself; he labels himself 'serious' and as a result he will then think about himself this way, and this is the way he will then feel and act.

I told him about the ACE card and asked him to think about what fun means to him. 'Doing things that give me pleasure is the simple answer,' he said.

Such as?

'Being entertained – I like to listen to live music, go to shows, comedy; I like to be at family gatherings where there's lots of laughter – those kinds of things would be high on my list.'

I then asked him to actually write these things down and try to be willing to have fun, and to be enthusiastic about it.

He smiled. 'Discovering new things, visiting places I've always wanted to see and making music would all be good fun.'

Our 15 minutes was up but already he had become more aware of himself, and the need to change. I arranged to have another 15 minutes with him the next day and asked him to think about arranging something fun that he would commit to.

When we met up and set the clock I quickly noticed that his ACE card had been working well! He'd arranged to take his family to see the Severn Bore, one of Britain's few truly spectacular natural phenomena.

'I've wanted to take my family there for years!' he said. 'I've also decided that I want to make music – have lots of instruments around and learn all the computer stuff that goes with it. That would be fun. And I really want to sleep outside under the stars now and again!'

Rob came a long way in a very short time! In committing to just two 15-minute sessions he changed his life for the better.

SUMMARY

It's easy to get the balance between work and play wrong or neglect our spiritual and emotional well-being, especially when we are living busy lives. In this chapter we looked at how to use the 15-Minute Rule to redress the balance and improve your sense of wellbeing.

12

CONCLUSION

'A journey of a thousand miles starts with a single step.'

Chinese proverb

As you have discovered while reading this book, the 15-Minute Rule has the potential to change your life, yet the concept is simple: the hardest part of any task is getting started but you can do anything for 15 minutes.

Your first 15-minute session is the starting, single step on your journey. Whether it leads to a completed tax return, a tidy house or a life-changing career move, it has the power to banish procrastination and set you on the right path.

CASE STUDY: DAPHNE

'The first thing I used the 15-Minute Rule for was my VAT return. I set the timer on my phone and just got on with it. I soon realized you can get so much done if you ignore everything else, which I wouldn't usually do. Normally I would hear the phone, pick it up; see an email pop up and take a break. But because I knew I had limited time I kept going.

'When the buzzer went off I was so keen to keep going that I set the timer again and did another 15 minutes.

'I knew also that apart from my VAT return I had to go out at a certain time that day – I had to be at an important meeting with clients and couldn't be late but afterwards I had friends coming round for supper. I found myself thinking in 15-minute intervals. I thought, OK, I'm going to spend 15 minutes on the washing, 15 minutes tidying up and that will leave me 15 minutes to wash my hair and 15 minutes to put my make-up on. And on each of these occasions I didn't deviate when anything else came into my path. And then you can have another 15 minutes where you can do all the catching up, all the things you couldn't do while you were doing the 15 minutes. Brilliant!'

Although she wasn't sure if it was OK to do a second 15 minutes straight after the first one, she remembered that flexibility is essential. She used the 15-Minute Rule in a way that suited her best. As you should, too. The only reason I suggest stopping after the first 15 minutes is to give yourself the message you can trust yourself to stick to the time frame. You need only begin with 15 minutes. There is absolutely no pressure whatsoever to carry on.

The influential psychologist Carl Rogers once said, 'What is my goal in life? What am I striving for? What is my purpose? These are questions which every individual asks himself at one point or another, sometimes calmly and meditatively, sometimes in agonizing uncertainty or despair. They're all old, old questions which are asked and answered in every century of history, yet they are also questions which every individual must ask and answer for himself in his own way.'

What would you dream of doing if you knew you couldn't fail? I urge you to follow the 15-Minute Rule on this fundamental question. It will change your life. Some of us set goals for ourselves and strive for them; others just evolve. Either way, we really do need to think about the big questions sometimes. One of the greatest gifts we have is free will: the gift of choice.

How many times have you gone round and round in circles knowing, again and again, that something in you, or your life, has to change? And then suddenly, the penny drops from your brain into your heart.

We can encourage more of these insights into our hearts by using the 15-Minute Rule, which helps us take action in small, manageable time frames.

'Progress is impossible without change, and those who cannot change their minds cannot change anything,' said George Bernard Shaw.

So now you are ready to be launched into the world. Thanks to your willingness and enthusiasm to embrace something new, you now have the 15-Minute Rule and a brand new set of skills to help you achieve the life of your dreams.

The 15-Minute Rule will take the gloom, doom and despondency out of all those horrible jobs that you've putting off and which have been bringing you down. Having unfinished business that we know we should attend to is extremely tiring. It's such a weight to carry around. But now you know how to split them into small chunks to make them easier to tackle, starting with 15 minutes and extending the time only when you have mastered the method and it suits you to do so. With this knowledge you release that negative energy and find the fun in following the 15-Minute Rule. You are going to feel so awake and alive again. You will have so much positive energy for all the exciting stuff that is coming your way.

This is where you can take the 15-Minute Rule to a higher level and start using it to find your purpose, release your potential and strive towards making your dreams come true. You have other tools now also, to work alongside the 15-Minute Rule. Apart from your willingness and enthusiasm, you have your ACE card (Attitude Changes Everything), the Power of Three, the strength of the settled decision and the wisdom of knowing spiritual harmony is available to you.

So, now you have everything you need, what are you going to do to change your life? When are you going to start? Do you have 15 minutes to spare, right now?

ACKNOWLEDGEMENTS

With many thanks to Fritha Saunders for her wise guidance, Alison Maloney for her good editing and to friends, family and my dog Billy for their love and support. I love you all.